István Szent-Iványi
Quo vadis Hungaria?

Originally published in Hungary:
Szent-Iványi István, Quo vadis Hungaria?
Kalligram, Budapest, 2018
© Szent-Iványi István, 2018
Translation © Andy Clark 2020
Translated from the Hungarian by Andy Clark

Book layout by György Harsáczki
Cover design used the painting of Caspar David Friedrich,
Wanderer above the Sea Fog

ISBN 978-615-80276-7-0

Published by Republikon Intézet Kft
1026 Budapest, Harangvirág u. 7.
Responsible publisher Péter Hann

István Szent-Iványi

Quo vadis Hungaria?

Where is Hungary heading?

Foreign policy dilemmas and strategic vision

Republikon Institute
Budapest

To my children, Klára, Ágnes and Domokos

Table of Contents

Part I.

The fundamentals

Who are we, and to where do we belong?

Who is Hungarian? What is Hungarian? These questions have long occupied the scholars of domestic intellectual life. Poets, writers, politicians, linguists, historians, ethnographers, cultural historians, and the representatives of who knows how many respectable disciplines, have agonised over this. In my opinion, there's no clear-cut answer to this; there's no uniform, consensually accepted definition of what it means to 'be Hungarian'.

The partial answers which each discipline provides can help us, and indicate the multifaceted nature of the question, but they don't bring us any closer to our goal of a precise definition of the concept.

Linguists classify our language as belonging to the Finno-Ugric language family, although this kinship is only clear to them; lesser mortals don't truly sense the kinship between Hungarian, Finnish, and Estonian languages.

Today's Hungarian language bears the traces of the enrichment effects of numerous other languages. We have a good number of newcomer words from Turkish, Slav, Latin, and German, and during development of the language, through the newcomer words and the so-called 'Germanisms', perhaps the German language has had the most significant influence on the development of today's Hungarian literary language.

Genetic research on ethnic origin has yielded surprising results. Based on the study of genetic markers, the closest kinship was shown to be with the Slavic peoples of Central Europe, and not necessarily those with whom this would be obvious. According to this research, the accuracy of which, of course, I cannot vouch for, our genetic markers aren't closely related to the Slovaks and Croats living with us, but rather to the Ukrainians and Poles.

There is still a debate among Hungarian scientists about Hungarian ethnogenesis. Of course, the point from which we can talk about the Hungarian people at all, is also a matter of debate. Perhaps there is a consensus that the Hungarian conquest, or the period immediately preceding it, is when we can already describe our (ethnically, probably very diverse) ancestors belonging to different tribes and tribal associations, as being Hungarians. But the ethnogenesis of today's Hungarians didn't stop here. It merged with the peoples found in the region, largely Slavs, maybe even Avars (if any of them remained after Charlemagne's campaign in Pannonia), then the later settlers (Cumans, Jasz, and then Franks and Italians, and an increasing number of Romanians, Armenians, Jews, and many, many others.

Ethnographers and cultural historians are can't give a clear answer to this question either. For a long time, the pentatonic-scale characteristic of our folk music was considered one of the determining factors. Undoubtedly, the pentatonic scale is characteristic of old-style Hungarian folk songs, and in our environment, is only characteristic of Hungarian folk music, but neither is it a special Hungarian peculiarity, also being widespread in many other parts of the world. We're rightly proud of such fine examples of Hungarian folk art as the cifraszűr (a traditional peasant folk-art-embroidered coat) or tulipános láda (wooden chest decorated with tulip motifs). Many sought to discover the reflection of the Hungarian people's soul in these, but we are bound by objectivity to state that these also have forerunners and similar instances with other peoples.

A long list of examples could be cited but they don't bring us any closer to our goal. These are all important components of our cultural heritage and part of our identity, but they don't – either alone or collectively – answer the question posed. Namely, because when it comes to being Hungarian, it isn't substance which is decisive, but the relationship to being so.

Whoever declares themselves to be Hungarian, assumes our cultural heritage, our traditions, and our past, is Hungarian. It's a highly complex legacy, and not every detail is easy to identify with. Our heritage doesn't just comprise of heroes, geniuses, and outstanding achievements, even though we have a tendency within us (as do other peoples) to accept only these. There is also a part of this heritage which has for a long time been a burden for us to bear. The history we live with, the unprocessed past, including decades of communism, the terror under Szálasi, the holocaust, or even the Horthy era, the assessment of which is still hotly debated. The glorious and less than glorious events of our history together form the medium that shapes us and made our people who we really are. The visible or presented part of identity is about what we want to be, or at least what we want to see ourselves to be, but deep down there are also factors that we keep silent about or that we'd prefer to forget.

Why is this at all important for our foreign policy? Just as identity is inseparable from the individuality of every human being, so foreign policy must be aware of who it represents and what traditions it is based on. Irrespective of whether you wish to free yourself from these very traditions, or to continue and fulfil them. If we wish our foreign policy to have character, depth, and not just comprise of a shallow surface, we need to be aware of these issues as well. We will only have a clear vision, a strategic vision of our country, if we know who we are and our relationship with ourselves is clear.

A distorted self-image leads to distorted politics: nationalism is always based on a biased self-image and on false myths. Excessive nationalism is one of the greatest threats to the stability, prosperity, and future of our region. We Hungarians aren't immune to this either. Notwithstanding that we have suffered so much in recent turbulent centuries because of our own nationalism and that of other nations.

This is why I am advocating that Hungarian foreign policy thinking consider the message of Count Miklós Zrínyi in his work (1660-1661) *Né bántsd a magyart* ('Don't mistreat the Hungarians'), which is still valid today: "We are not inferior to any nation". This can be the alpha and omega of the relationship we have with ourselves: we don't consider ourselves different and superior to anyone, but neither do we suffer from an inferiority complex, because we know that we are no less worthy than any other nation. Thus, we can avoid the Scylla and Charybdis of foreign policy: the dangerous excesses of nationalism, and the adoption of servility and self-capitulation which stem from a sense of inferiority.

We have no reason to follow our great poets, from Dániel Berzsenyi to Endre Ady, in living our Hungarianness through constant self-flagellation, but we must also refrain from allowing our insights to be blinded by way of self-praise and massaging of our ego.

If we already know who we are and possess a healthy, balanced relationship with this, should we not also take a look at where we belong, where our place is?

It isn't only the past, traditions, and historical and cultural patterns which are an essential component of the country's foreign policy identity, but also where we classify ourselves, where we *really* belong, and where our place is in the world.

In geostrategic thinking, it's common wisdom that geography also determines our destiny (Geography is Destiny). This is, of course, a rough simplification, there being no clear definition, but there's no doubt that the geographical environment (which isn't primarily to do with topography or hydrography but does cover this) also has a significant impact on a country's foreign policy. Foreign policy strategy mustn't be detached from the geographical situation, especially with its political implications.

The home of the Hungarians lies in the Carpathian Basin, our wider environment being Central Europe, that is, slap bang in the middle of the continent. The wind-battered countryside of the Carpathian Basin wasn't called the peoples' highway for nothing, it being a meeting place and melting pot of different cultures and civilisations. Prior to the Hungarians arrival, no people settled permanently or formed a state in this landscape. Our thousand years' survival is a serious achievement deserving of respect, but the geographical location of our chosen homeland, hasn't proved hugely favourable.

Our homeland, the Carpathian Basin, is part of Europe. Europe is a vast geographical area, in de Gaulle's generally accepted view, spreading from the Atlantic to the Urals, but we can also say that it's a gigantic peninsula of the even more vast continent of Eurasia. This geographical area has been divided into several regions down through history, and its borders are still very much alive despite the process of European integration. We can talk of Eastern and Western Europe, but also of the North-South axis, the centre, and the periphery, and of Central Europe, which has its own identity. All of these units can be substantiated, verified, and further divided into subregions. Yet there seems to be a historical-cultural dividing line in Europe which is stronger than any other. This dividing line runs roughly along the line between Western and Eastern Christianity. Western Europe ends at the point where Gothic, Renaissance, Humanist, reformation, and enlightenment ideas reached. In the other half of Europe these haven't been felt at all, or if so, only belatedly, indirectly, or in an ephemeral way. These roughly determine the specific differences between the two major historical cultural regions of Europe.

The excellent Hungarian historian Jenő Szűcs correctly pointed out that it's in Central Europe that the defining character-

13

istics of the continent's western and eastern halves often mix and occur in a form which is not pure. He describes our Central Europe as an intermediate region, characterised by a desire to belong to the West in its ambitions, but also one which in its cultural-societal make-up, shows many oriental features. Hungary is illustrative of this intermediate region, but this is also true of Poland, Croatia, the Czech Republic, today's Slovakia and even, to a certain extent, the western half of the Habsburg Empire. In his work *Kompország*, Endre Ady metaphorically describes Hungary's ambivalent identity, as the country not belonging anywhere, and oscillating between the civilised West and the barbarian East.

Geography doesn't clearly align us on the issue of our affiliation: we're roughly equidistant from the two great regions, so our affiliation isn't the result of a geographical determination but a conscious decision. Hungary's more outstanding leaders consciously chose a Western orientation during our historical turning points. Following initial uncertainty, Saint Stephen very consciously tied his country firmly to the Western world. He embraced Western Christianity, requested a crown for himself from Rome, took a wife from Bavaria, and invited a multitude or priests, monks, and soldiers to Hungary from the west in order to consolidate this strategic choice. The Kingdom of Hungary clearly became part of the Western world, although it straddled its eastern borderlands. Our country not only accommodated, but also provided fertile ground for the intellectual and cultural currents arriving from the west: Gothic art (the peoples who settled in Hungary, primarily the Saxons, were a great help in this, of course), the renaissance, the ideas of humanism, and every important trend in the Reformation even reached the easternmost part of the country at that time. Later, the ideas of the enlightenment also had a noticeable effect on us. The forerunner of the dominant ideas of the 1848 revolution was also of

Western origin: equal rights, equal sacrifice theory of taxation, freedom of the press, and freedom of speech. The trauma of losing World War I and the ensuing unjust Trianon peace treaty cast this Western orientation into uncertainty but didn't succeed in turning our country completely against it. Our best scientists, writers, poets, artists, and intellectuals have never denied our country's western identity. Following World War II, the intention to belong to the West was again reaffirmed, and this certainly would have been the country's natural orientation had it not been prevented by the Soviet occupation and forced Sovietisation. The October 1956 revolution was also a heroic attempt to shake of the yoke of the East and regain liberties which, if won, would have had the natural consequence of joining the West. Eventually, the change of regime in 1989-90 provided an opportunity for this, and Hungary, like its fellow former Eastern-Bloc neighbours, grasped it firmly with both hands. This choice was confirmed by the results of two referendums held in the past twenty-five years (in 1997 for NATO membership, and in 2003 for EU membership). Even the hundreds of thousands who have sought their fortunes abroad in recent years have all gone to the West, because it was seen as offering an attractive socio-economic model.

The west isn't simply a point on the compass, but a successful socio-economic and political model. Hungarian foreign policy must be committed to this affiliation because I am convinced that it is in Hungary's national interest to unequivocally belong to the West.

In recent years, government policy has sought to re-orientate Hungary's foreign policy. This experiment was dubbed the Eastern Opening policy. This policy has become a kind of state ideology, which wasn't primarily about the otherwise welcome diversification of the Hungarian foreign economy, nor about the necessary broadening of foreign policy thinking, and broadening its horizons, but about creating the ideological basis of the illiberal state.

The Eastern Opening policy has three pillars: an ideological one, a foreign policy one, and a foreign trade one. The latter is the least important and most unsuccessful one of them. The ideology's foundations were laid by Russian politician Vladimir Surkov, and Russian political analyst Alexander Dugin, also known as Putin's Rasputin and who calls it Eurasiansim. It purports that the West is decadent, is in constant decline, and is becoming nihilistic. Liberal democracy is an outdated way of organising a state, is unable to respond to the challenges of the age, and which strong leaders need to replace with strong states which rely on the people. The solution is an illiberal state which rejects the values of distorted liberal democracies and protects traditional values; the familial holy trinity of God, Home, and Family.

The Eastern Opening also has an important foreign policy pillar: to strengthen relations with other illiberal states and eastern despots, to strengthen economic and political dependence on these countries, and at the same time weaken the Western system of relations, the institutions of Western cooperation; the EU and NATO. This foreign policy is constantly on the attack, criticising the Western partners an especially the organisations which support deeper integration, actively seeking conflict with them. At the same time, it flatters and compliments the Eastern states and offers them a nonsensical strategic partnership. It dresses all this up under the disguise of sovereignty, concealing it by the catchphrase of it being an independent, autonomous foreign policy.

I am convinced that the policy of Eastern Opening in this form is the completely wrong direction for Hungary to take, and if we don't deviate from this path in time, it could result in some very serious consequences. At the same time, it's an excellent illustration of foreign policy in so far that if it is in sharp contrast with the country's historically established identity, natural orientation, and values of its citizens, then it entails some very serious domestic and foreign policy risks and could plunge the country into a pointless and even dangerous adventure.

Nothing irreparable or irreversible has happened so far, but the chances of this do exist in the uncertainty of the current orientation. Hungary therefore needs to turn back from this dead-end as soon as possible and return to among those whom we truly belong. Our culture, our history, our traditions, and social patterns are all tied to the Western part of Europe; in a broader sense, to the Western world. This is what Hungarian identity tells us with regard to our much more historically, rather than geographically, defined sense of belonging.

Does Hungary have a mission? (Should it?)

The question is somewhat of a red herring in that no country has a mission that can be established on the basis of objective criteria or external perspectives. There are many countries though, whose people or leaders believe that providence has entrusted them with a special task that is their duty to fulfil. We can cite thousands of examples of this throughout history: the leaders of the Soviet Union believed (at least for a fairly long period of the existence of the USSR) that their mission was to spread the ideas of communism worldwide and ensure they prevail. The Third Reich also had a sense of mission: to create world domination for the Aryan nations, and within that primarily for the German 'race'. It's not only totalitarian regimes and tyranny that have a sense of mission, though. The dominant ideology of the British Empire was one of liberal imperialism: the co-called 'white man's burden'; that is, the spread of superior civilisation among the 'primitive peoples', and their 'elevation' to the level of British civilisation. We also have a present-day example of this. The United States has, until recently, had a sense of mission according to which, as an 'indispensable nation' it has a sacred duty towards democracy, the protection and spread of human rights, and to act against repressive tyranny.

Mid-sized and small nations tend to consider their global duties in more modest terms, but that doesn't mean that quite a few of them don't believe in their own exceptionalism or their selectness. We Hungarian's aren't strangers to this either. During the

Austro-Hungarian Monarchy, many believed in Hungarian supremacy, in the pre-determined superiority of Hungarians over the peoples living with them. The Hungarians were considered a 'gentlemanly people', a race born to reign, and the nationalities living alongside us were disregarded and looked down upon. During these times our country was rightly called the land of mirages, which rushed blindly into the tragedy of World War I in the fever of an imperial dream of thirty million Hungarians. The interwar period saw imperial dreams replaced by the Klebelsberg ideology of 'cultural superiority', which although somewhat more modest in its ambitions, continued to believe that Hungary could once again become the leading country in the region as well as a mid-ranking regional power. Representatives of the ideology didn't pay too much attention to convincing the other peoples living in our environment why it would be beneficial for them, thus, apart from us, with few exceptions no one even supported our coveted regional mid-ranking power status. There wasn't even any need for bind faith; the will of providence and the Hungarians historical right, sufficed.

The crushing defeat in World War II, which for a short time threatened to make even the existence of Hungary as an independent country a realistic possibility, put an end to the dreams of a Hungarian mission for a long time. Forty years of occupation, the loss of its de facto independence, and its Sovietisation precluded the formulation of a new independent mission. Communist leaders servilely followed Moscow's instructions and refrained from even appearing to create a distinct independent foreign policy profile. In part, they did this for ideological reasons: they were internationalists who slavishly accepted that the leading power of the socialist camp was the Soviet Union, and that they had a duty to fall into line in almost all matters, be it the quashing of the Prague Spring or the boycotting of the 1984 Los Angeles Olympic Games. The truth is that not all communist leaders followed this path. Tito's Yugoslavia, *Ceaușescu's Romania, and Enver Hoxha's Albania followed a different foreign policy path. It's also true though, that none of these countries were under Soviet occupation, whilst all the Soviet-occupied nations (in addition to Bulgaria, but there are historical reasons for this: the Bulgarians viewed the Russians as being Slavic brothers liberating them from Turkish occupation) constantly aligned themselves to the Soviet position. On the other hand, sober realism also advised them to do so, them being well aware that dissident communist leaders such as Imre Nagy or Alexander Dubček faced the wrath and cruel revenge of Moscow, and that didn't augur well. As a result of the beneficial effects of Gorbachev's perestroika, Hungarian foreign policy began to gain some independence in the second half of the 1980s. Initially, the creation of a new, now independent foreign policy identity proceeded just with baby steps, gathering pace only later. From here on we can talk about a truly independent Hungarian foreign policy, and the differences characteristic of the Hungarian foreign policy stance can be understood not only as small tactical steps, but also as real strategic objectives.*

It was during this period that Hungary became a driving force of the transformation of Central and Eastern Europe, a key actor in East-West rapprochement. All this was reflected very spectacularly in foreign policy. This was the most visible showcase of domestic political processes in the world. Hungary was the first communist country in the Soviet Bloc to re-establish diplomatic relations with Israel, South Africa, South Korea, and Chile. It joined the UN Geneva Refugee Convention, the Alps-Adriatic Working Group, and embarked on the process of joining the Council of Europe. Hungary decided to allow East German refugees free passage to the West, initiated negotiations on the withdrawal of Soviet troops, and in the spring of 1990 the then Foreign Minister, Gyula Horn, raised the issue of Hungary's membership of NATO (albeit in a somewhat controversial manner when he proposed that Hungary simultaneously be a member of NATO and the Warsaw Pact).

Although no one expressed it in ideological terms, Hungary had, by the end of the 1980s, an easily identifiable and marked role in world politics. We could even call it a mission, should we so wish. Hungary was a key player in the great transition, the individual steps of which had a serious impact on international politics as a whole. We could state that in 1989 – 'the year of miracles' – Hungary was punching well above its weight in terms of its influence on the development of world historical events, as compared to its own size and economic power. It became a kind of alignment, a reference point, an example to follow for many countries in the region. (I'm primarily talking about Hungary now, but there is no doubt that Poland played at least as much a role in the transition at the time, but Poland has a much larger population, so given its size, Hungary's influence is still noteworthy.)

It would be unfair to hold the Hungary of today accountable for the loss of this privileged and exemplary role, which was also accepted by others. It was the consequence of a special historical moment and situation which, being realistic, was never going to last. It's true though, that neither was it politically expedient to completely squander the political and moral capital accumulated at the time, within two decades.

The task of Hungarian foreign policy should have been one of preserving this valuable position for as long as possible, or at least saving as much from it as possible.

In the early 1990s our political capital was still more or less well-managed. Hungary became – in 1990 – the first country from behind the Iron Curtain to join the Council of Europe. Hungary was the initiator and motor behind the dissolution of the Warsaw Pact in 1991, and the establishment of the Visegrad Group the same year. In 1994 it became the first to apply to join the European Union. These were all steps which inspired the countries of the region, and our partners among those countries undergoing democratic transformation, followed suit.

We had the chance of maintaining the role of being (one of) the model countries of the transition; a mission, if we like. However, this promising role was overshadowed by two unfavourable circumstances: one foreign-policy related; the other domestic-policy related.

Unfortunately, with the passing of the year of miracles, the demons of the past were revived: nationalism strengthened throughout the region, Hungary included. To the south a bloody civil war broke out, in the newly independent Slovakia under Mečiar and in Romania under President Iliescu, nationalism became the state ideology, and these voices gathered resonance in Hungary, too. It was difficult to keep up the appearance of a model country whilst having constant disputes and quarrels with most of our neighbours. Hungarian foreign policy attempted to take the lead by concluding a series of bilateral basic treaties, but this didn't meet with great success (the Antal government concluded the Hungarian-Ukrainian Treaty in 1991, the Hungarian-Slovenian Treaty in 1992, and the Hungarian-Croatian Treaty in 1993, and then the Horn government continued this in 1995 with the signing of the Hungarian-Slovakian Treaty, and in 1996 with the Hungarian-Romanian Treaty).

Another factor also adversely affected Hungary's international and thus regional standing: the difficulties of Hungary's transition, especially its failures in the field of economics. Whilst in the early 1990s the whole world considered our country to be destined for success, by the middle of the decade we'd lost that favourable image. In early 1995, the country was on the verge of state bankruptcy, whilst the transition was accompanied by extremely severe social shocks. More than a million jobs were lost within the space of just a few years, the standard of life even fell below that of the Kádár era, crime rocketed, corruption showed itself across the board, and privatisation brought with it a series of dubious deals. The regime-change promise of a better livelihood was shattered, and the initial success story envied by others, struggled to keep its head above water.

As a result of these two factors, the nimbus that had earlier characterised Hungary weakened, and we slowly but surely slipped back from being a role-model to being an average transition country. Fewer and fewer wanted to follow our example, and even fewer viewed the Hungarian model as a success story. Nevertheless, in 1997, together with Poland and the Czech Republic, we were the first to be invited to join NATO (although our geographical location and the U.S. air base in Taszár did play an important role in this), and in 1998 at the EU summit in Luxembourg, we were ranked among the prime candidates, the 'Luxembourg six', albeit our accession in 2004 was as part of a larger group of ten.

Thereafter, the backsliding was continuous. Steadily deteriorating economic performance, domestic instability after 2006, and then the 2008 global financial crisis which brought the country back to the brink of bankruptcy, definitively scuppered our plans of being a model state. It's true, though, that at the time we didn't yet face the risk that we might even become pariahs within the EU. We had to wait a few more years for that.

In the decade and a half from the mid-1990s until 2010, primarily for the reasons just mentioned, Hungary's ambition of having some sort of mission was almost completely lost to public thinking. Hungary needed all of its strength that remained after the increasingly harsh internal battles, to stay afloat, and thought increasingly less about, and had less reason to, be proud of its own performance.

2010 was also a clear dividing line in this respect. The new government, led by Prime Minister Viktor Orbán and with a broad election mandate, even promised a new beginning in foreign policy. Orbán sought to erase the past, in which he himself had been an active participant, not only in domestic politics, but also in foreign policy. He announced an ambitious foreign policy activism in the first year of his rule. He made no secret of the fact that acquiring regional leadership was something close to his heart, nor that he also wished to take on some kind of international leadership role. This had a slogan-like catchphrase of 'Let's dare to be great!', likely a response to a statement mistakenly attributed to former Foreign Minister László Kovács, "We're small-fry". The slogan accurately expresses the government's voluntarist philosophy that "we're as big as we imagine ourselves to be". The basis of this move is purely will; appearance and communication are everything. The goal of achieving the status of a mid-ranking regional power, which has a long history in Hungary, has also been redefined.

Government communication constantly drums it in that Hungary is a strong and successful country, and that others look at us with envy. We're already ahead of the game and are once again becoming a model state thanks our leaders having a good sense for where the world is heading and embarking upon a path that the others will later be forced to take too. Our mission is a fight for freedom against Brussels in defence of the powers of the nation state, because the Europe of the future cannot be federal, only a Europe of nations; that is, through governmental cooperation.

For a long time, this strategy seemed doomed to total failure. Hungary has also become increasingly isolated within the EU, receiving continuous reprimands and lectures, and its performance (despite loud propaganda to the contrary) hasn't given rise to any special recognition, us having been ranked somewhere mid-table among EU member states, but in the bottom-third regionally.

Then, the 2015 refugee crisis – which undoubtedly put the EU to the test, and in this the EU certainly fell a little short – came as a heavenly blessing for the strategy. The time came for the mission of building a previously unsuccessful freedom-fighting and illiberal state to be replaced with a new mission: the defender of (Christian) Europe, who will arrest and reverse the influx of mostly Muslims from the East. It's undeniable that Viktor Orbán recognised the potential weight of the refugee crisis and its expected impact on public opinion very early, at the beginning of 2015. He consistently built his strategy upon this foresight, which turned out to be correct. Although he was fundamentally wrong when he predicted a year of rebellion in 2017, he hoped that it would completely redraw the political map of Europe and elevate leaders like him everywhere. Although this didn't maerialise, he saw well that this crisis would have serious domestic political consequences in many member states, and that it would also increase his role in the world.

Today, therefore, the Hungarian government's foreign policy has an openly assumed mission of playing a leading role among countries that refuse to accept refugees.

The question now is whether this mission is good for us. How does Hungary benefit from it? From a governmental perspective, of course, it makes sense, is at least somewhat beneficial. In domestic politics it brings tangible benefits, as a significant part of Hungarian society agrees with and supports this situation – not least due to massive and manipulative government propaganda. It also has foreign policy benefits because it eases isolation, is a connecting point with other governments (for example, it's the main field of cooperation among the Visegrad Four) and establishes the Hungarian government as a factor to be taken into account on the world stage.

Still, my opinion is that in doing so, although the government gains something in domestic politics, Hungary loses a great deal. The change in the international climate in relation to asylum seekers is only beneficial to the government on the surface. Hardly anyone can, or wants to identify with the extremism, exaggerated anti-EU sentiment and the callous treatment of asylum seekers that characterises Hungarian refugee policy. Many agree with the Hungarian government that any mass and uncontrolled influx must be halted (even in the case of real refugees), but there is no longer any consensus in terms of methodology or rhetoric. Furthermore, it's unlikely that the topic of the refugee crisis will permanently dominate public discourse and public opinion. The traumatic experience of 2015 and 2016 may fade after a while if there isn't a similar wave of asylum seekers. It' already noticeable that this topic is slowly losing its relevance. The public is no longer primarily concerned with this, but with other problems (digitisation, automation, climate change, pandemic risk, etc.) in which Hungary has nothing worthwhile to say. However, if this issue doesn't remain one of the most important topics of concern for the public, then everything that played a role in Hungary's handling of this matter (rhetoric, callous treatment, lack of solidarity) may come to the fore.

In any case, we won't be much better off with this role, even if those who really do hold similar views to our government about asylum seekers come to power in many European countries. Because these like-minded people don't only reject asylum seekers, but all foreigners, including our citizens, whether as workers or students. A good example of this was the short-lived governance of the Austrian Freedom Party (FPÖ). When it came to asylum seekers, there was complete agreement with the Hungarian government, but one of the first measures taken by the former Austrian coalition government was to restrict family allowance payments for non-Austrian workers. The Austrian government is also pushing for a reduction in the burden on net-contributing

EU member states; meaning less money for countries eligible for the Structural Funds and the Cohesion Fund.

The Austrian government is also far from alone in this, given that the populist parties of Western Europe are all also very narrow-minded about EU subsidies and would be happy to radically reduce financial allocations. It thus won't do Hungary much good if our government is at the forefront of a movement which would indirectly restrict the rights of our citizens and severely curtail the financial resources available for our catch-up. This mission is, in our case, distinctly self-destructive, and in stark contrast to our interests.

If this mission is harmful, do we actually need any mission at all?

I believe that we do. It's no coincidence that every major company, firm, or association today, formulates its own mission statement.

I believe that we need to go back to our roots, but also adapt to the challenges and requirements of the 21st century. Hungary's new mission must be decided not a by a narrow elite, but by wider society which is interested in public affairs; not only political parties but also economic actors, the academic elite, and representatives of civil society must be involved in the elaboration of the mission.

In my opinion, Hungary's mission is based on its commitment to democracy, the rule of law, and a free market economy. Hungary is part of the West, a constructive and solidary partner. Our task is to strengthen the value community of the Western world, to consistently represent its values. If the community to which we belong is strong and successful, then we also benefit.

Respect for minority rights is an important element of European values, something we have good reason to be advocates of. We can only fulfil this role credibly if two conditions are met. At home, we ensure full equality of nationalities; not only on paper but also in reality and, in the international arena, we don't deal with the issue selectively; we not only act in defence of the rights of Hungarians outside of Hungary's borders, but also fight for the respect of minority rights in general and endeavour to solve the problems of other minorities. If we do this, others won't consider us as nationalist troublemakers but defenders of European rights, and at the same time we can thus best ensure the rights of Hungarians living outside of Hungary's borders.

Hungary directly borders the Western Balkans. What happens there also affects us. This region is an important market and investment target area for the Hungarian economy; therefore it's in our basic interest to strengthen the region's democratic processes and stability and help the Western Balkan countries' integration efforts. Fortunately, we have something to hold onto, since we've also more or less consistently supported the countries of the region in recent years. Hungary has a favourable reputation in the West Balkans; there is demand for our experience and knowledge, and partners are open to our suggestions. Our mission is to be an advocate within the EU for the region's European ambitions and to help the integration process in the region as an EU ambassador. This role also serves both national and European interests.

Part of our mission is to build up the regional centre role of Hungary which will make our country one of the key economic, commercial, financial, transport, and cultural-intellectual hubs of the region. For a long time, this goal seemed to be at our fingertips, but by now, it seems ever-more distant, even if still within sight. Much is needed for this to happen: legal certainty, a favourable business environment, a modern education system, much better transport connections than at present, creative freedom in the fields of science and the arts, and a vibrant cultural life.

In recent years, many talented, especially young, Hungarians have left the country whom we desperately require for the implementation of a new mission. The hope that many people will return as a result of favourable changes that will take place and help us build a new European Hungary, is not baseless. After so many wasted years this will not be easy to achieve, but neither will it be impossible. This though, requires radical changes to both our foreign and domestic policies alike.

Values, interests, and the national interest

Among the wealth of literature on foreign policy thinking there has long been an unproductive, though by no means pointless, debate about the role of values and interests. As in most debates of a political nature, positions here are often polarised and simplified. The small differences tend to be exaggerated by the parties, who present nuances as being irreconcilable contrasts. The original home of this debate is the United States, where the two dominant large schools of foreign policy thought – the adherents of the idealistic and realist schools – have been debating the primacy of values or interests for many decades. The idealists are advocates of a value-based foreign policy, whereas realists see interests as being decisive. In reality, neither group completely denies the raison d'être of the other principle; it's the proportions which are debated. This is also natural, given that no country today pursues a purely value-based foreign policy, not even the United States, which has a hegemonic role. The opposite is also more or less true, but even though an interest-based foreign policy is more easily devoid of values, it's difficult to find an example of this in chemically pure form.

When we talk of a value-based foreign policy, it's primarily about weighting, and the order of importance of the factors which play a role in foreign policy decision-making. Thus, a value-based foreign policy doesn't mean that purely and only value-related considerations play a role in all decisions, but rather that decision-makers carefully consider the value perspectives undertaken each time and taking other factors (interests, external or internal constraints) into account, either endorse them or withdraw their endorsement. In countries where a value-based foreign policy is pursued, the value premises are openly undertaken and the actual foreign policy practice is always compared with the values undertaken; that is, it is also monitored on this basis.

Value-based foreign policy is often confronted by raw interests, and this is the real test of the sincerity of value-based foreign policy. A recent good example of this is the economic sanctions imposed on Russia following the annexation of Crimea. Germany is the main economic loser in this decision, but Poland has also been hit hard. Yet both countries have been prime movers behind the introduction of the sanctions, because this move followed on from the values they espoused. It could of course be questioned as to whether the decision was really made solely on the basis of values, contrary to their economic interests, or whether an important interest, a security and strategic consideration, also played a role here. They could have rightly believed that if Russia's aggressive expansion policy went unanswered, Moscow could see this an encouragement for further expansion, with Poland possibly being one of their prime targets; something which would also threaten German security interests. A similar scenario occurred during the Cold War, when the United States took on the primary guarantor role in a policy of 'obstruction'. The policy of obstruction can be deduced directly from the foreign policy's commitment to values; that is, the values of freedom and democracy, and the requirement to act against tyranny, but it served Washington's overriding national security interest at least as much, given that the spread of communism posed a serious security risk.

The examples presented also shed light on the fact that it often isn't possible to draw a clear line between values and interests; they are mixed, or a decision can be justified on both grounds.

The Kirkpatrick doctrine – named after Jeane Kirkpatrick, United States Ambassador to the UN and foreign policy advisor to President Reagan – sought to resolve the conflict of values and interests. According to the doctrine, the sum of values and interests is always constant in U.S. foreign policy, which means that where many interests arise, values play less of a role, and where there are no direct interests, values take precedence. This viewpoint leads us to the realist school (Kirkpatrick, incidentally, is considered an adherent), which basically attributes a secondary role to values. This school also has several centuries-worth of traditions and boasts highly noble ancestors, founding fathers of the theory including Nicoló Machiavelli, Thomas Hobbes, Prince Metternich, and the 'Iron Chancellor' Otto von Bismarck. They all held the view that moral considerations and ethical premises in political decisions – foreign policy included – were not only secondary but also explicitly harmful or unnecessary. There is no such thing as friendship or loyalty, just interest. This is expressed by Lord Palmerston's much-quoted adage, "We have no eternal allies, and we have no perpetual enemies. Our interests are eternal and perpetual".

According to the realists, decisions must be determined by interests, external and internal constraints, and other politically relevant factors. Politics, in their view, is not qualified by intentions but by results. Adherents of this school are also thus often referred to as pragmatists, whilst their critics call them unprincipled opportunists. It's precisely the greatest drawback of the realist or pragmatist school that it is separated from non-principle by a very narrow boundary which is often imperceptible at the time of action, which may be profitable in the short term but can backfire in the medium- or at latest, the long term.

The unprincipled opportunist is incapable of lasting alliances or collaborating in coalitions, because the had-hoc momentary interests often conflict with those of their political allies. In the eyes of others the opportunist is an unpredictable, unreliable partner who is ready to betray at any time.

Trump's foreign policy doctrine is considered to be one particular variety of this realist foreign policy. Based on his stance displayed during the 2016 election campaign, it's a transactionalist foreign policy based on bilateralism. This idea isn't simply pragmatic, but a give-and-take approach without strategy which examines each decision solely in the context of bilateral relations and in terms of immediate benefit. This is a completely new and somewhat risky approach which, fortunately, has only been partially transposed into practice and has not yet become the guiding principle of American foreign policy action. Foreign policy – like politics in general – is a continuum defined by continuous actions and decisions and not an aggregate of independent, isolated steps. Therefore, a foreign policy that makes individual decisions regardless of context, or of other previously- or later-planned, but still related, decisions, is doomed to failure. The trouble with transactional foreign policy isn't just that it's completely unprincipled, but above all, that it's incoherent, confusing, and unsuccessful. This is well-evidenced by the inconsistencies and failures of American foreign policy under Trump.

Hungarian foreign policy after the change of regime was conceived in the spirit of idealism, and it's thus understandable that it was initially strongly ideological and committed to values. At the time, this didn't only mean the rhetoric; it also manifested itself in concrete action. The country also needed this, because without it, it would hardly have been capable of carrying out with credibility the radical change, the complete reorientation of foreign policy, that the transition to democracy demanded.

Under the Horn government, the commitment to values remained, albeit – even if only down to the Prime Minister's personality – it was supplemented by strongly pragmatic features. Perhaps the most spectacular sign of this was that under the Antall gov-

33

ernment, eastern relations (I'm primarily thinking of Russia and China here) neglected also for ideological reasons, became more valuable, although not a priority, but did receive a role in the foreign policy agenda. Under the first Orbán government, ideological elements and thus adherence to values intensified, especially in the first half of the cycle, as demonstrated by foreign-policy leadership in the field of eastern relations, but also by Hungary's participation in the NATO peace-keeping operation in Kosovo.

On a rhetorical level there wasn't any change in the adherence to values after 2002, but a cautious correction in favour of pragmatism did begin as early as the time of the Medgyessy government. This was marked by the declaration of Chinese relations as being strategic, and then by the increasingly obvious rapprochement with Russia at the time. This was fulfilled in the eastern policy of the Gyurcsány government, although the foreign policy strategy adopted by his government still adhered to values, albeit this was already little more than lip service; empty nice words, whilst the majority of foreign policy decisions were defined less and less by adherence to values.

The true and clear turn took place after 2010, with the second, and even more so, the third Orbán government. Although the new foreign policy strategy adopted in 2011, and which was still had the hallmark of János Martonyi, reaffirmed an adherence to values and expressed the personal conviction of the Foreign Minister, in practice it diverged already from the offset, and after a while, openly turned against it. The policy of Eastern Opening proclaimed in 2011 clearly contradicted the declared principles of the foreign policy strategy adopted at the same time (a commitment to Western values), after which the announcement of the victory of the pragmatist revolution wasn't long in coming. It happened in 2014, when Prime Minister Viktor Orbán, in a strategic keynote speech at a meeting of Hungarian ambassadors, stated that "ideologically centred foreign policy guidelines were invented for half-witted countries by smart countries". Regarding this, he explained that his main expectation when it comes to diplomacy is that it promotes economic interests. This stance was supported by numerous steps taken in Hungarian foreign policy, such as the infamous Ramil Safarov case, when the government returned the Azeri axe-murderer back home in exchange for hoped-for benefits. Incidentally, the case is a good illustration of the complete failure of such politicisation: not only did this move cause much moral damage (Armenia severed diplomatic relations with Hungary, and as of yet they haven't been restored), but the much hoped-for Azerbaijani kick-backs haven't materialised either (albeit according to some, there have been, it's just that they haven't benefitted the Hungarian budget).

Opposition leader András Schiffer, who slated Hungarian foreign policy as being 'wheeling and dealing', wasn't far off the mark. Indeed, our foreign policy is currently an incoherent series of ad-hoc relations and actions without a clear strategic goal, lacking a well-defined focus of action, and which stands at the crossroads of raw pragmatism and unbridled opportunism.

From what I've written so far, it's clear that I'm a believer in the value-based tradition, but neither am I in favour of naïve idealism. In order for us to once again be an esteemed partner, respect for, and the prestige of Hungarian foreign policy, must be restored, and this cannot be achieved on a purely pragmatic basis. This requires a clear set of values and a clear-cut relationship with them.

I'm aware that no country in the world today pursues a purely value-based foreign policy, not even the great powers have the opportunity to do so, and especially not a medium-sized country with limited ability to assert their interests. A desirable Hungarian foreign policy is based upon a reasonable reconciliation- and delicate balance of values and interests, avoiding the pitfalls of naïve idealism and unbridled opportunism. We can draft this balanced approach pliably in such a way that in our foreign policy we can't always do what we should do based on our values, but we must always follow our values when we have the opportunity to do so.

Foreign policy involves a special category of interests, an ace in the pack; so-called national interest. Debates on national interest go back decades, and it's in this debate that the most extreme points of view clash. Some even deny its existence, whilst there are those who believe that the national interest is the indispensable foundation of any rational (meaning realist) foreign policy. Some only use this rhetorically, but this even has an elaborate theory behind it, taught in universities and the subject of many doctoral theses.

Throughout history, many have abused the concept, and it has generally been used to legitimise foreign policy actions. As an extreme example, Hitler also wanted to justify his conquests on the basis of national interest, but this is what China is now referring to in its expansion into the South China Sea, and Recep Erdoğan has also launched a punitive strike against the Syrian Kurds. These cases aren't worth wasting too many words on, as it's obvious that these references to the national interest aren't based on theory but use the rhetorical persuasive power inherent in the concept, for reasons of domestic policy as well as legitimacy. If something is in the national interest, then its opponents are obviously enemies of the nation as well. Thus, whoever monopolises the use of the concept of national interest, acquires the 'right' to equate their opponents as enemies and traitors of the nation. It is particularly common on the part of nationalist trends, movements, and parties, that they present themselves as being owners of the national interest and vindicate the right to determine the national interest and even use the concept itself as a weapon against their political opponents. There's no deeper theoretical consideration behind this; it's much rather a technique of power which abuses the lack of consensus on the content of what constitutes the national interest. Incidentally, one branch of the realist school came to the conclusion that since national interest cannot be precisely defined in terms of content, we can in fact consider the goals pursued by the current government to be the national interest. This though, brings us to the conclusion that there's no such thing as national interest, only a government with a temporary authority to lead the country, whose foreign policy aspirations can, if we so wish, even be called the national interest.

A good example of this interpretation is the practice of the current Hungarian government, which prefers to identify the national interest with its own objectives; that is, it arbitrarily names its current power interests as being in the national interest. This is undoubtedly a convenient solution for the current government, but this interpretation precludes the possibility of using the term meaningfully.

Hans Morgenthau, one of the defining apostles of realist foreign policy thinking, called the promotion and assertion of the national interest a fundamental task of foreign policy. For the realists, the national interest plays roughly the same role as the adherence to values does for idealists: it's the alpha and omega of action, it's the main motivator and legitimator of foreign policy action. Morgenthau of course also encountered the difficulty of defining the concept of national interest in terms of content. He considered the survival of the nation to be the main national interest, which includes the security of the nation, the preservation of its identity, its prosperity, and its territorial integrity. In his view, this is the primary aspect that foreign affairs politicians must consider in every decision and subordinate every step to minimising the threat to the national interest and maximising the potential benefits to the national interest.

It can be seen that at the abstract level it's easy to build such a consensus on the content of the national interest: perhaps everyone agrees that it's an important national interest to preserve the country's sovereignty and territorial integrity, guarantee the security of its citizens, promote prosperity, and prevent threats and risks. The difficulties begin when these abstract and consensual values are put into practice or asserted. At this level it's much more difficult to build a broad consensus right away and talk about national interest based on it. The same goal can be also approached in many ways, different tools and tactical considerations can result in different action plans even for the same goals. The question arises as to whether the national interest can only be applied to a distant and abstract goal, or also to the path we choose to achieve that goal.

For the above reasons, the concept of national interest should be treated very carefully. It may be useful in foreign policy analysis as an analytical tool, but it carries great dangers if it's instrumentalised and viewed as a weapon of political struggle. When we come across this interpretation, we always look at how arbitrary its use is. We can only consider it appropriate to use the term if what we call the national interest is based on a kind of consensus agreed by the main players in the political spectrum, but by all means with broader political and societal support than just from the governing parties, and which represents not just momentary, but longer-term interests. National interest is of course not independent of time, circumstances, or external factors. It is thus not eternal, but neither is it by any means momentary, nor exclusively serving or reflecting the momentary interest of an identifiable part of the political spectrum.

In the field of foreign policy, I consider it essential to have ongoing, systematic consultations between key political actors and a common effort to identify consensual goals. I am aware that this isn't always possible, and that the government must act even if the efforts to reach a common position fail. A responsible government will make these efforts in any case if it truly believes that it's a matter of identifying or asserting a genuine national interest.

When we talk about the role of values and interests in foreign policy, we can't fail to talk about the moral dimension of foreign policy. This can, of course, be easily remedied by the fact that foreign policy is subject to the same moral rules as politics in general. According to popular and, in Hungary, especially popular views, politics (foreign policy included) is basically an immoral activity to which moral rules do not apply at all. As widespread as this view is, it's certainly a misconception. Like all human activity that can be described by rules, it has its own morality. Without this, it would be a completely unpredictable, chaotic and self-destructive activity. If the parties and participants weren't bound by any moral rules, there would be no point in alliances or agreements, as no one could trust them to be abided by (violation of the rules is, of course, still common).

The question, of course, is not only whether political actors have any morals, but whether the moral-based judgment of politics is at all a relevant perspective, whether it makes sense to morally examine the motivations for political action, or only on the basis of utilitarianism; how useful and effective the given policy is.

For me, Max Weber's neo-Kantian approach in his study *Politik als Beruf* (Politics as a Profession) is still valid today. Weber, who for a short time himself took on a political role at the dawn of the Weimar Republic in one of the German liberal parties, is clearly of the view that politics also has ethics, and that politics can be judged on its own ethical rules. Weber contrasts the ethics of conviction (Gesinnungsethik), which call for the assertion of moral values based on the actor's beliefs and intentions, with the ethics of responsibility (Verantwortungsethik), which we can call the ethics of responsibility for the consequences as well as the benefit of the community represented by the politician. According to him, the politician shouldn't follow the traditional ethics of belief, but the ethics of responsibility, and their activity should be judged on this basis. He himself sums up the moral dilemma inherent in this: *"Only he who is sure that he will not collapse, if from his point of view, the world is too vile for what he wants to offer it, and despite everything is capable of saying: 'even so!' has a calling for politics."*

All this can also be formulated in the categories of ethics of intent and consequence: political activity is thus basically judged not from the perspective of intentions, as we know that the road to hell is paved with good intentions, but from the perspective of consequences. This however, also raises awkward questions about the nature of politics: can this be interpreted as meaning that the goal sanctifies the means, and only the outcome matters? I don't think so at all. True, in politics the goal sometimes upholds the use of tools that are unacceptable to everyday morality, but this doesn't entail that all sorts of tools, without limitation, can be used in the interest of a 'good purpose'. This is because the tools may discredit the noblest of goals to some extent, and it can come about that the damage caused by the tools may far outweigh the hoped benefits of the right goal. The use of immoral means may also call into question the correctness of an otherwise morally justifiable goal. Therefore, the common saying that success cannot be disputed, is not true either. Success can be highly debatable from a moral standpoint, and success alone does not morally justify the use of immoral means. Therefore, it cannot be upheld that the consequences and the results justify all, which is why Weber argues that there is a need for the politician's sense of responsibility and his – emphasised with good reason – 'rule of thumb' (Augenmass), sense of proportion, which guides us in setting goals for ourselves which are morally correct, and that when selecting tools we take care that they don't undo the moral correctness of the goals.

Foreign policy strategy

The basis of a successful foreign policy is the adoption and follow-up of a clear and realistic strategic plan. Without a strategy, foreign policy action is just constant improvisation and haste. In his work *The Art of War* – often still quoted after two thousand five hundred years – Chinese military strategist and scholar Sun-Tzu claims that "Strategy without tactics is the slowest way to victory. Tactics without strategy are just chaos before defeat." It's hard to disagree with him. Our failures in foreign policy prove the wisdom of the ancient author. Foreign policy built on ad-hoc tactics is doomed to failure. This is true even if we have to say that Helmuth von Moltke, a German military man of the high nobility, was right when he claimed that "I do not know of any war plan that survived the moment of encounter with the enemy." Indeed, in delicate situations and under unpredictable circumstances, strategies don't work in their original form; they must be reconstructed creatively to adapt to the constantly changing situation. This, however, doesn't at all mean that that the time and energy spent on developing the strategy was unnecessary. The circumstances under which a certain encounter with the enemy takes place, matter: how prepared we are for the moment when we can no longer cling rigidly to the original ideas but must constantly re-plan our steps based on the foundations laid.

Sceptics who reject strategic thinking happily refer to American professional boxer Mike Tyson, who boasted that anyone can have a plan for him, until he lands a good punch. However, this only worked for him so long as he was much stronger than his challengers. Probably in highly unequal struggles, the disproportionately stronger party needs less of an elaborate strategy than the one who wants to succeed with limited resources. It suits us to be modest because we aren't a resource-rich country. We can only be successful if we have a realistic strategy in place and are willing to follow it in a disciplined manner.

Even in the hegemonic world power that is the United States, it's an unwritten expectation of the president that in the first year of their presidency they adopt a national security strategy which is broad in scope but should include the foreign policy strategy of the new administration. All presidents do this, although there is no doubt that the strategies put forward are generally subject to fierce criticism and torn apart, not only by political opponents, but also by the academic elite and think tanks. This even happened recently with President Trump's strategy, but critics weren't much more lenient with Obama's national security strategy either.

Where we are concerned, in terms of foreign affairs strategies, if we look only at the documents that have been adopted, we aren't too badly off. In the past decade or so, the government in power has even adopted three foreign policy strategies:

– In 2008, the MSZP-SZDSZ government's Hungarian foreign relations strategy.
– In 2011, the Fidesz-KDNP government's *Hungarian Foreign Policy after the EU Presidency* strategy, and finally
– in 2015, the new foreign affairs leadership's Foreign Trade and Affairs strategy.

We can essentially only talk about the first two, because all we know about the most recent strategy is from statements, as it has no publicly available text. Also, the only thing worth saying about the first two here is that unfortunately both of them have already expired. Both would have deserved to have been tried in practice, but neither of them had the good fortune to do so. The first strategy, adopted in 2008, was preceded by a serious professional debate and consultation. The academic elite, recognised external experts, and NGOs involved in foreign policy, were also involved in the proposal, which was discussed with opposition parties and, in fact, adopted as a result of a long, careful, drawn-out process. It could be said that the process of adopting the strategy was exemplary. The great merit of the strategy is that, for the first time, it covered foreign relations as a whole; that is, not simply foreign and diplomatic tasks in the narrow sense, but also trade and cultural diplomacy, and popular diplomacy too. The only major shortcoming that can be attributed to it is that in practice they were no longer able, nor truly wanted, to put into practice the novel objectives of the strategy.

The situation is very similar with the foreign affairs strategy presented in 2011 by the Ministry of Foreign Affairs led by János Martonyi. It's an interesting, valuable document containing acceptable goals, but this wasn't tried in practice either. Martonyi announced the strategy of Global Opening when Viktor Orbán had already set the strategic goal of Eastern Opening for Hungarian foreign policy. Behind the aspiration for Global Opening, which is more appealing to me, was the intention that Hungarian foreign policy would go beyond its usual Europe-centric limitations and diversify its activities geographically. It didn't designate any privileged point of the compass as opposed to the Eastern Opening, and there was no sort of ideological implication behind it. The Global Opening wasn't intended to replace, but to complement, the previous clear Western orientation of Hungarian foreign policy.

Given that the main directions of foreign policy weren't determined by the Ministry of Foreign Affairs during this period

43

either, in the period immediately following the adoption of the strategy, alongside the rear-guard fighting for the Global Opening, the Eastern Opening increasingly came to the forefront as a strategic direction.

The current strategy, the Foreign Trade and Affairs strategy, was announced by the Ministry of Foreign Affairs leadership in 2015, and several press conferences and presentations were held on it, but the text of the strategy hasn't been made public since then. As a result, critics aren't in an easy position, because they can only deduce the content of the strategy primarily from the statements of the Prime Minister and the Foreign Minister, as well as from foreign policy initiatives.

It's clear that the words 'foreign trade' don't come first in the title of the strategy just by accident. The new foreign policy is clearly subservient to economic interests, the traditional foreign policy activity playing a secondary, subordinate role in the strategy. It can be concluded from the statements of Viktor Orbán that he's a believer in the extremely pragmatic, realist school of foreign policy, which is why he's also accused of unbridled opportunism by his critics. Whist Martonyi even claimed, which of course wasn't necessarily true even then, that Hungarian foreign policy was primarily value-based, Viktor Orbán openly stated at the ambassadorial meeting in 2014 that *"Ideologically-based foreign policy was invented by smart countries for half-witted countries"* and asserted that his government didn't follow *"a foreign policy which always focuses on the issue of values"*.

If we consider this to be one of the strategic foundations of Hungarian foreign policy, we can state that at least this principle has been faithfully followed by our foreign policy.

The new strategy not only modified, but simply terminated the consensus that had continuously defined Hungary's foreign policy orientation since 1990. Even József Antall, the first freely elected Prime Minister and Géza Jeszenszky, his government's

Minister of Foreign Affairs, laid down three main directions of Hungarian foreign policy action in the White Paper adopted in the autumn of 1990: Euro-Atlantic integration (i.e., Western engagement), good neighbourly relations, and responsibility for Hungarians living abroad. There have always been different emphases in the interpretation and practical approach of these three directions, but until 2010 no one doubted the correctness of the system of objectives as a whole. During the time of János Martonyi's Ministry of Foreign Affairs, strong correctional attempts were already perceptible, but the domain of a foreign policy based on consensus had not yet been eliminated. The real change came after 2014: the true reorientation in foreign policy can be felt since then. The clear attachment to the West has been replaced by some kind of obscure 'bridge role' between East and West, and the so-called 'peacock dance'. A spectacular rapprochement has begun between Hungary and Russia, not only in trade but also the field of politics. Hungary has also developed close political relations with China that go far beyond economic rationality and interests. Orbán continued his policy of spectacular rapprochement, with illiberal Turkey and many other authoritarian, repressive regimes. At the same time, he distanced himself from his Western allies, launched a meaningless and unnecessary 'freedom struggle' with the institutions of the European Union, and came into conflict with the United States, Germany and many other key partners. The last move was most likely not an intended goal, only an inevitable consequence of the new strategy. The corrective capacity of Hungarian foreign policy is weak; it doesn't correct errors but adds new ones.

I make no secret of it that I believe we need a new, comprehensive foreign policy strategy. The primary goal must be to restore Hungary's clear Western orientation, improve the country's international prestige and standing by demonstrating constructive, cooperative and predictable behaviour, and thereby strengthen

Hungary's international ability to assert its interests, contribute to increasing our security, international economic success, and the country's rise. It is of course, not enough to set lofty goals; the strategy must also set out how it shall be implemented in the changing international environment. And even this won't suffice, because it's also necessary to create the conditions and the system of tools required for its implementation.

This strategy must be born of an open, transparent debate process in which all stakeholders must be invited to participate. Political parties, NGOs, think tanks, academic experts, analysts and foreign policy journalists. Full consensus is most likely an illusion, and in any case isn't an aim, but to have a general consensus in relation to at least the main objectives, is. In some respects the current situation is analogous to that of regime change: the country's foreign policy needs to be radically reprogrammed. Thus, the main aspects of the strategy shouldn't be aimed at one political cycle, nor simply reflect the programme and aspirations of one or a few political parties but be based upon a much broader consensus than the current policy.

This book is intended to be a modest treatise and a contribution to the necessary and urgent task of the hoped-for redesign of Hungary's foreign policy strategy.

The myth of sovereignty

The rallying cry of 'sovereignty' is now in season. It's long been popular in Hungary but is also gaining ground in Europe, too. There are few concepts that have undergone so many changes in meaning as sovereignty has during its long history, and which today has many different interpretations, often contradictory not only in terms of nuance but also in substance. It isn't my intention to give a detailed overview of the history of the concept, but a brief outline may shed light on the relativity that can also be seen in today's use of the concept.

If we research the origin of the concept of sovereignty, we can go as far back as Marcellus Ulpius, a Roman jurist who lived in the 2nd century, whose works have not survived, but whose position can be reconstructed from the writings of his followers. If I interpret correctly the message that reaches us through multiple references, he was the first to regard the emperor, the unconditional lord of the Empire, as sovereign; that is, the holder of the supreme power not controlled by others. He laid the foundations of the position which prevailed until the end of the Middle Ages that we consider not the nation, country, or empire, but a person, prominently a ruler, as sovereign, whose unlimited power is not limited by earthly compulsions and over whom, in principle, stands only God. This, of course, was only theoretically true, since this power wasn't unlimited either, even in developed feudal societies. Certain laws (the Magna Charta, Golden Bull, etc.), the feudal aristocracy's privileges and institutionalised representative bodies, and later the influence of the estates of the realm, set a limit to the 'unlimited' exercise of power by the sovereign ruler.

Thus, at first, it was eroded in practice, and then the prominent thinkers of the enlightenment also spiritually undermined the idea of sovereignty that had prevailed for a millennium and a half. It's thanks to the Enlightenment that the sovereign was toppled from the throne, both literally and figuratively, and the people were endowed with unlimited power. From then on, we see the people as a source of legitimate power; no one can deprive them of this valuable property, albeit the people can delegate their natural right to their representatives, from whom, however, they have the right to take it back at any time.

John Stuart Mill, as would be expected of a true liberal, didn't find the true holder of sovereignty in the collective but in the individual. For him, it's not the abstract concept of people or country, but the self-determination of the individual that is the legitimate source of power, so for him the autonomous personality, the individual is the real sovereign. People's sovereignty is the result of many, many individual decisions; the sum of individual sovereign decisions.

The development of the concept followed a somewhat different path in international law. The decisive turn is rooted in the spirit of the Peace of Westphalia (1648), which ended the Thirty Years' War. An important antecedent of the Peace of Westphalia was the Religious Peace of Augsburg (1555), which stated that "cuius regio, eius religio" (who owns the territory, sets the religion). This laid the foundation for true autonomy and unlimited sovereignty over the formerly heavily dependent and subordinate electoral princes. The Peace of Westphalia set all this in stone, and for centuries the basis of the international order, laying the foundations for territorial integrity (in other words, the inviolability of borders) as well as the principles of non-interference in internal affairs.

These were, of course, postulates that have been violated many times throughout history; one could say that they were ignored many times rather than respected. Yet these became internationally accepted, accountable rules that worked flawlessly until such time as a strong challenger to maintaining the international order arose, and who hoped to profit more from flouting those rules than from adhering to them. To this day, the UN has stated that its mission is to maintain this order, although we can see that its efforts are not always accompanied by success.

No matter how much failure surrounds adherence to these principles, it isn't mere naivety or lofty idealism to cling to them. It's still better to uphold these principles as a rule than to give them up in frustration and expose the world to the law of the jungle or the right of the strong.

Modern international law associates sovereignty not with individuals and not even with peoples but, by default, with countries. There is general agreement that today the sovereignty of a country is constituted by the combined presence of four components. A country is considered sovereign if it exercises its **authority** over the **entire population** of a **given territory** alone and without restrictions and is **internationally recognised**.

This is, of course, a textbook case, albeit it applies to the vast majority of UN member states. Life, though, produces countless awkward exceptions.

History has many examples of the international community recognising a country as sovereign, of course in most cases, rather, a government, which holds no sovereignty over its own territory or population at all. During World War II, there were a number of émigré governments (especially in London) that were considered sovereign by the Allies, who concluded international treaties with them although they exercised virtually no sovereignty over the territory and population of their own country. For a long time in the Western world, the Republic of Taiwan was considered the sovereign government of all of China, even being a permanent member of the UN Security Council between 1946 and 1971, despite that their actual authority only extended over the island of Taiwan, a fraction of the size of the behemoth China. Several countries consider the Palestinian National Authority as being the representatives of a sovereign country, even though it has only very limited authority over the territory – recognised by many countries – it oversees. There are a good number of countries, a part of whose territory is under permanent occupation and foreign rule, yet we consider them sovereign. Here are just a few examples from Europe: Cyprus, Moldova, Ukraine, and Georgia.

Nor does international recognition provide clear guidance on these issues, although extreme cases don't provoke real debate. In general, we don't question the sovereignty of countries who are recognised by most countries in the world. The other extreme is represented by 'countries' that aren't recognized by anyone, or just by a small number of nations. In their case, it's self-evident that we should doubt real sovereignty. Such instances include the Turkish Republic of Northern Cyprus, which is only recognized by Turkey, or Abkhazia, Transnistria, South Ossetia, and Nagorno-Karabakh, which are still recognized by only one, or a few countries.

The sovereignty of Kosovo, which has so far been recognized as a sovereign state by 117 countries (i.e., the vast majority of UN member states), is also a really tricky issue, with two important permanent member states of the UN Security Council (Russia and China), as well as several EU member states (Spain, Romania, and Slovakia) still not recognising it as an independent state. Thus, it isn't only the number of countries who give recognition, but also their composition, which is of great importance.

Thus far, we've talked about the formal criteria of sovereignty; it's now time to also assess the issue in terms of content.

Is there any sovereignty at all in today's globalised world that is consistent with the original meaning of the term? In other words, is there a country that can limitlessly assert its interests without external coercion? I contend that the classical exercising of sovereign power in this absolute form, as suggested by the legal definition, never existed, and is even less possible in our modern world. That is, no country is able to assert its interests without taking into account external and internal pressures and constraints. Of course, the capacity of each country to assert their interests differs greatly, depending largely on their economic performance, system of alliances, military capabilities, the readiness and effectiveness of their diplomacy, as well as their geostrategic position. It's clear that the United States possesses a very strong ability to assert its interests, but the experience of recent years has also shown that this capacity has very strong external and internal limitations. The strategic failures of American foreign policy clearly showed the boundaries that even the world's leading power couldn't cross.

Many believe that dictators have more freedom of action; that is, sovereignty, than the governments of democratic states because at least they don't have to reckon with internal constraints (public opinion, the opposition, the constitution, and so forth). Kim Jong-un's room for domestic political manoeuvre is indeed greater than that of any democratically elected leader, but he will likely have to face some internal resistance. This is indicated by frequent bloody showdowns within the system. While he constantly tests the international community's patience with nuclear experiments, he's careful not to go too far. Internationally, his room for manoeuvre is somewhat limited, it being a matter of survival and constantly taking care that his provocative steps don't lead to the collapse of his system. Thus, his sovereignty is only strong in theory; in practice it is, in fact, extremely limited.

51

Sovereignty by no means provides unrestricted scope for foreign policy action, but is highly relative, limited by a number of external and internal factors. There are also very important internal constraints on the scope of foreign policy action. In a democratic state governed by the rule of law, the government acting on behalf of the state must take into account the expectations of the public, on which the independent media, nowadays ever more so social media, opposition parties, NGOs, and civil society organisations, have a serious impact. A frequently cited example is the story of the withdrawal of the French Republic from Algeria, or the failure of the United States in Vietnam. Neither of them suffered defeat on the battlefield, but rather, were forced to lay down their weapons as a result of public opinion back home. Sovereignty may be limited by the constitution or certain constitutional decisions (for example, Germany's Basic Law sets very strict conditions for the use of military force in other countries, whereas constitutional rules in some neutral countries preclude the joining of a military alliance and, in Japan, constitutional restrictions are in force with regards development of the military, and so on).

Yet the real limits of sovereignty are primarily external. International law, as well as international treaties, albeit within very narrow limits, mark the room for manoeuvre of each country. This room for manoeuvre is, of course, largely determined by the economic performance, military potential, system of alliance or lack thereof, and geostrategic position of the given country. The content and scope of sovereignty are influenced by the historical past, traditions, cultural and social patterns. So, there are so many different components to sovereignty, but no one has unlimited sovereignty.

Membership of international organizations entails – albeit to varying degrees – obligations; that is, restrictions on sovereignty. Some international organizations, such as the UN, Council of Europe, the OSCE, the OECD, the WTO, and so on, lay down rules which are binding, or even sanctionable on their members, which, of course, the members voluntarily undertake and incorporate into their internal legal system, meaning that the limits of their scope to manoeuvre are clearly defined by those rules. This is even more true of organisations pushing for integration, most notably the European Union, which originally started as an intergovernmental organisation but is now on its way to becoming a loose federal state. The EU's regulatory activity also covers areas that were previously the exclusive competence of the nation-state, and it has thus became the main standard-setter, primarily in the field of economic life. Its regulations are directly applicable in the member states, are legally binding, and nor do they require publication by national law. It's no coincidence that European sovereignists see the EU as the number one enemy and that their main objective is to regain national sovereignty; to place European-wide competences within the competence of the member states.

Even in professional articles and studies, we often come across the misleading wording that, by joining, the member states have relinquished part of their sovereignty and ceded it to the EU institutions. This, however, isn't true, because with a few exceptions, no part of their sovereignty has been relinquished or transferred to the common EU institutions, but some of their sovereignty has been exercised jointly with the other member states. The importance of an individual member state decision is indeed diminished, but, on the other hand, the same member states are given a say in decision that affect other member states; i.e., they are part of the sovereignty of other member states. It's a case of swings and roundabouts. All this significantly compensates them for the loss that they suffer in certain areas. I emphasise here that it isn't the impersonal EU, but the community of member states that make the decision, jointly with MEPS elected in the member states.

53

All these examples also prove that the complete, textbook sense of, we could say, ideal-typical sovereignty, in today's world is a mere illusion. But that doesn't mean that the concept doesn't have a magical appeal, sometimes a hypnotic effect on public opinion. The concept of sovereignty as a rallying call, a mobilising buzzword, is experiencing a renaissance again today. Bringing this concept to the fore is a symptom of a crisis – it's popular because we face dangerous challenges and severe crises; feelings of vulnerability and helplessness create frustration, dissatisfaction with existing conditions grows, and people seek a quick cure for trouble.

Roughly a hundred years ago, the fall of the Weimar Republic was preceded by such a public mood, and it's no coincidence that one of the defining slogans of the era and the battle cry of the far right sounded eerily similar: it was also about the idolisation of sovereignty. There were, of course, highly understandable reasons for this, as the Peace of Versailles effectively deprived Germany of many attributes of independence, and part of its territory was under foreign occupation and another arbitrarily demilitarised by the victors. In this situation it was a perfectly reasonable and legitimate attempt to restore national independence, which, for understandable reasons, was pursued by the entire political spectrum, from the Social Democrats to the Liberals. Thanks to the efforts of the ingenious German Foreign Minister Gustav Stresemann, through negotiations, Germany achieved great success in restoring sovereignty in the sense of international law, although this wasn't the case in all areas.

This, however, didn't satisfy the masses feeding the messianic expectations of sovereignty. Because by then, sovereignty was no longer simply a matter of national independence but a desire for mythical power, a reparation to the German people for their defeat and humiliation.

There has also been a prominent theorist of this notion of sovereignty among conservative thinkers, in the person of legal scholar Carl Schmitt.

Schmitt found the roots of sovereignty to be in the will. Whoever wants something and achieves it by way of a command, is sovereign. Therefore, only the power that has the right to declare a state of emergency and is able to exercise it; that is, it can carry out its will through orders without restrictions, can be considered sovereign.

Sovereignty was also a key issue for the National Socialists. Hitler speaks in *Mein Kampf* about the acquisition of unconditional sovereignty, which he interprets as based on the ability to self-sustain (national autarchy), and the possession of significant living space that provides military security. Sovereignty, he said, is the privilege of the big and the strong; even talking about the sovereignty of small states is ridiculous.

The concept of sovereignty endowed with metaphysical content didn't just play an important role in Germany. It was a central concept everywhere in the far-right movements of the era, from Action française to Italian fascism. It's certain that the myth of sovereignty and the abuse of this myth itself contributed to the terrible tragedy of World War II which for a long time discredited the mythical interpretation of sovereignty, at least in Europe. During the Cold War, the East-West confrontation created a fault line and posed a threat that also overshadowed the extreme interpretation of the concept, as it would have weakened the cohesion or defence capabilities of the Allies. On the other hand, the external threat had a very beneficial effect on reconciliation and coalition-building, and integration efforts.

Today, sovereignty is re-emerging as a buzzword to which nationalists, populists, eurosceptics, and anti-globalists; that is, all those who have a hostile attitude to the values and institutional system of liberal democracy, react sensitively. The strength and viability of liberal democracy has always been demonstrated by allowing unrestricted self-criticism, choosing open debate with its opponents, and incorporating the lessons of debate into its system through its self-correcting mechanisms. We could reassure ourselves that liberal democracy has successfully coped with the myth of sovereignty once before, so why would it be any different now? This is a rather optimistic assertion, because at the moment this fight isn't going particularly well. Using the slogan of 'sovereignty', the Leavers won the Brexit referendum in 2016, the far-right everywhere – from the French Rassemblement national to the Dutch Party for Freedom, to the German AfD – is attacking the EU and, of course, the traitorous elites, citing lost sovereignty. The Hungarian 'freedom struggle' against Brussels uses very similar intellectual ammunition, and the anti-EU rhetoric of the Polish government is also based on this. The list of examples could unfortunately go on and on, but these are sufficient to prove that the myth of sovereignty has awoken from its slumber and is ready to wrestle power from the hands of 'traitorous and corrupt, nationless, global elites' and place the sacred relic of sovereignty on the altar of unconditional national independence.

As elaborate and rhetorically well-structured the sovereignists' critiques are about the current situation, so vague and uncertain is the offer that their followers promise. What will happen if they win? Why will it be good, and to whom will it be good if it is so?

I'm not going to deal with individual domestic policy proposals here now, suffice to say that they're diverse and often contradictory; perhaps all they have in common is that they are generally unrealistic.

The situation is different with regards the sovereignists' foreign policy vision. In simple terms, they believe in the Europe of nations and reject everything that goes beyond strictly intergovernmental cooperation. The main enemy is naturally the idea of a federal Europe, but even the current level of integration is unacceptable to them. They agree that a significant part of the competences exercised jointly should be returned to the competence of the nation-state, but there is also a debate among them as to exactly which ones.

It's clear that the concept of a Europe of nations corresponds best to the period from the Peace of Westphalia until World War II and which was based upon a balance of power between European powers. Involuntarily, the question arises: was this situation really that ideal? Didn't it lead to two terrible world wars, genocide, and widespread suffering? Didn't this period have the obvious lesson of getting over it through integration? Did not these lessons lead to German-French reconciliation, the Schuman Plan, and then the Treaty of Rome establishing the European Economic Community?

If we really want to get back to that, Brexit is the guiding model for us. Let's face it, leaving is the only real, compromise-free return to the nation-state framework. Britain is following this scenario by leaving. We have no experience of the long-term effects of Brexit yet, but the risks can already be assessed. It's no coincidence that to this day the camp of those who condemn Brexit is very strong.

Not all sovereignists are pro-Leavers, although almost all of them also toy with this idea. Eastern sovereignists, not least because of their financial opportunism, don't at all want to leave, because they desperately need the massive financial transfers which they are entitled to as members. What they really want is an á la carte European Union, where rights are not accompanied by real obligations and everyone voluntarily decides what they undertake from EU legislation or values. At the same time, they don't want to give up the financial support because they're aware of the serious consequences for the national economy. It's easy to understand the meaning of this position, which is basically based on national selfishness, but it's hard to agree with it. Why would it be in the interest of the net contributing member states or those who don't benefit from the EU coffers. They didn't create or later join the European Union to access additional budgetary resources, but to promote their economic, political, and cultural interests and protect and uphold and defend their values. What sovereignists propose isn't therefore, an attractive alternative for the others; there's no reason to seriously consider it, let alone accept it.

Taking a step forward, what if the idea of sovereignty comes to power in all or many EU member states, including the dominant major member states?

This is certainly the worst-case scenario for us. It would lead to the immediate disintegration of the European Union, with all its negative consequences.

As is often the case in board games, back to square one from which the whole integration process started. Keep in mind that integration started because the model that preceded it went bankrupt. Or even in this instance, it's conceivable that the formal disintegration of the EU wouldn't happen automatically, but its meaning would certainly be strongly questioned, even by Eastern sovereignists and freedom fighters. Because if these sovereigntist forces come to power in most member states, including the net contributors, they'd probably quickly put an end to the generous cohesion policy and support systems, and the real losers would be *exactly* the eastern member states. A good example of this is the Austrian coalition government, of which the FPÖ was a part, and the former Italian government, in which the Lega Nord played an important role, the efforts of both governments being aimed at reducing and reformation of financial support available to eastern member states.

This isn't yet a direct and present danger, but we can no longer speak of it as if it doesn't exist at all. These risks should be considered by Hungarian foreign policy, and action planned based on lessons learned.

According to the English idiom, if you're digging a hole for yourself and want to get out, don't dig any further. If we can accept that the strengthening of the sovereignists camp in Europe is not in our interest, then it isn't right to be its standard bearer and place ourselves at the helm of this confused movement.

Many of us also have reservations, in principle and related to values, about the myth of sovereignty, and especially about those profiting from this myth, but this isn't necessary for us to realise that this current view of sovereignty is a myth that's harmful and dangerous to us for pragmatic reasons. Even if we can't learn from our past, we should at least try to interpret and decipher the tendencies of the present. Our history teaches us that when we built our foreign policy on myths and illusions, we always failed. We finally have a chance to win now, but only if myths, the myth of sovereignty included, don't obscure our vision.

It's my conviction that Hungarian foreign policy in the 21ˢᵗ century must be based on the patriotic concept of national independence, respect for our traditions, the nurturing and preserving our values, and a sober representation of our interests. Hungary won't receive the greatest benefit by reiterating this at every step, but by being able to create a healthy harmony of our interests and values and representing them consistently, free from illusions.

Part II.

The world which surrounds us, and us, Hungarians, within it

Strategic vision – the world order in which we live

Today's world order

You may have good reason to ask what kind of world order we're talking about when one sees only crises, conflicts, and dangerous challenges around us. Wouldn't it be better to talk about world disorder instead?

Well, world order in the absolute sense, that there would be order, harmony, and heavenly peace in the world, has never existed, and in spite of utopian dreams, it probably never will exist. Yet it isn't meaningless to speak of a 'world order' in the limited sense that there is an international system based on written and unwritten rules, as well as the sanctioning of rules that normally settles conflicts and designates the legitimate room for manoeuvre of individual states. We can only talk of this since the world became global, which came about at the end of the age of discovery. This far preceded globalisation, which is a story of only a few decades and which, thanks to the info communication revolution, connects the inhabitants of our planet through full simultaneity and a multitude of interdependencies and interactions.

The ancient Pax Romana didn't constitute a world order, as its rules extended only to the then known borders of the Western world, had little knowledge of the world beyond its borders, nor did it have any effect on it. The heyday of the Roman Empire and China's Han Dynasty roughly coincided, both of which were hegemonic powers in their own known worlds, but since they had no knowledge of each other, we can't speak of interactions or dependencies. In our present terms we can say that before the global world, there was no unified world order, but parallel regional orders.

Perhaps the first de facto world order after the Napoleonic Wars was Pax Britannica, created by the British Empire and which covered the whole of the world then known outside Europe. This, of course, didn't mean that the British Empire ruled the whole world, nor even that it was able to enforce its will on all matters important to it, but that the most important pillar, and sanctioner of violations of this world order globally, was the British Empire. There were written and unwritten rules that also applied to the British Empire, and these rules were essentially rooted in the Peace of Westphalia that ended the Thirty Years' War. Adherence to these rules was ensured by the European balance of power, whilst globally this order was defended by Britain, which ruled the seas. This system was of course by no means perfect and wasn't particularly long-lived. World War I had already signalled a severe crisis in – and the twilight of – the status quo, followed by a protracted agony and, finally, the bloody and devastating World War II which placed the final nail in the coffin of a world order based on a European balance of power. This, in part, greatly weakened and made the European superpowers a secondary factor, the two world wars having already proved that they couldn't guarantee any reassuring order, not only for the world, but even for themselves.

This was followed by the so-called bipolar world order based upon the real winners; the United States and the Soviet Union. Some experts believe that this was when the so-called liberal world order, of which only the first and longest phase so far rested on the balance of power between the two poles, followed by a unipolar phase based on the hegemony of the United States after the end of the Cold War, came into being. I, on the other hand, share the view that the bipolar and unipolar alignments represent two separate, fundamentally different world orders. That is, they aren't two stages of the same era but two historically distinct periods. This terminological debate though, doesn't affect the explanation's further substantive claims.

The European superpowers became secondary, supporting actors in this new alignment. Germany, defeated and divided, was no longer a force to be reckoned with, but Great Britain and France were also greatly weakened, coming out of the slaughter of World War II having lost their great standing. In the post-Yalta world of influence, order was maintained by the military, primarily nuclear, balance of power between the United States and the Soviet Union. This ensured stability and security for nearly four decades, the two superpowers 'keeping order' in their respective sphere of influence and settling conflicts with each other according to agreed rules. Following the break-up of the Soviet Union, this balance of power was also upset, with successor-state Russia losing its superpower status and becoming a Eurasian regional power. Fortunately, all of this took place without major commotion or bloodshed.

Following the break-up of the Soviet Union and the deep internal crisis in Russia, an obvious consequence was a new, so-called unipolar world order. There was no other reasonable alternative to this then, because if this didn't happen, only global turmoil and chaos could have taken the place of an order based on a superpower balance of power. For a long time, Russia seemed to be reconciled to the new situation and its new status, and the United States undertook to expand its former role, the thankless task of being sole pillar of the new world order. This role not only involved serious financial sacrifices, but frequently came at the cost of much bloodshed, and additionally made the country and its citizens pretty unpopular in much of the world. It's no coincidence that while there was a long-standing general consensus amongst the U.S. political elite about its role as a pillar, the public became increasingly less enthusiastic about it.

The pillar of any world order can only be a superpower with very significant financial resources, outstanding military potential, and a sense of mission. For a long time, all three conditions were present for this in the United States. The new world order proclaimed the supremacy of the values that formed the basis of American identity, but also the public treasure of all Western civilization. The political model advocated for the new arrangement was liberal democracy, and its economic model was the free market economy, especially the dominant role of free trade. It is also the holy trinity of the state religion of a globalised world, where the role of the holy spirit is played by free trade: the free flow of goods, capital, and services (and, within certain limits, people).

This didn't of course mean that the United States could do what it wanted without constraint, and that everything turned out as would have been most favourable for it. Many examples prove that this was far from the case. The United States and its allies suffered many failures and setbacks after 1989, but no one fundamentally compromised their security, their most important interests were successfully defended against all challengers, and the rules they established were generally enforceable. Since the end of the Cold War we've been living in a world order that's comfortable and homely for the countries of Western civilisation, serves its interests and security well and, until recently has provided general stability.

This new golden age, however, lasted a very short time. The first major wound it suffered was the 2008 global financial crisis. This showed the economic foundations of the current international order to be fragile, self-destructive, and that the corrective mechanisms don't work well. Doubts over the omnipotence and supremacy of globalisation and modern capitalism have intensified in countries that are clearly privileged and beneficiaries of the globalised world. The crisis destabilised the most developed countries, but it also provided encouragement to the system's victims, critics, and also reappearing challengers.

However well this world order worked for a decade and a half, it wasn't at all perfect and not everyone was happy with it. Not everyone welcomed the place they were given with joy and gratitude, and the rules that the prevailing power and its allies had established for the others were also increasingly called into question. Sooner than expected, challengers appeared on the horizon. For a long while, it seemed that these revisionist powers weren't yet strong enough in themselves to fundamentally overturn the current international system or take their place as *the* global superpower, but they had just enough strength to seriously disrupt its operation.

The challengers

1.) Russia:
Russia has been banging on the door for years, demanding half of the kingdom. In the 1990s it still appeared that Russia, struggling with many of its serious internal problems, was satisfied with the place it had in the new situation following the Cold War. For a long time neither its ability nor ambition encouraged it to change this situation. After Vladimir Putin came to power though, this attitude fundamentally changed. The country's new leadership left no doubt that they were dissatisfied with the country's position as a mere regional power. Through his aggressive and expansionist policies, President Putin has constantly tested the limits of his own room for manoeuvre, as well as the reactions of the pillar of the unipolar world order. His first clear attempt to test the outside world came in the summer of 2008

when Russia violated Georgia's territorial integrity by military means, and then permanently occupied part of its territory. The experiment was a success, the world reacting with uncertainty and half-heartedly to his flouting of the rules. This experience may have emboldened him to openly disregard the international system's agreed rules in the spring of 2014 with the annexation of Crimea and the military support of the separatists in eastern Ukraine. Nor did he hide the fact that he would henceforth be one of the challengers to the existing order.

The stability of the world order was ensured in part by the fact that relations between countries were framed by clear rules. Among these, respect for territorial integrity and the sovereignty of other countries was a particularly important rule. It was only acceptable to violate these rules with the authorisation of an international organization (mostly the UN) or with the consensus of key members of the international community. Examples of the latter are the operation in Kosovo, and the coalition attack on Iraq. In neither case was a UN mandate successfully obtained; in Kosovo, NATO members jointly decided to intervene, with the unanimous support of many other countries, whilst in the case of Iraq, the so-called Coalition of the Willing carried out the occupation of the country. Russia spectacularly ignored these rules in both 2008 and 2014, thus openly challenging international community norms. Military engagement in Syria aimed at propping up the regime of President Assad (and, of course, Russian military bases secured by his grace), which began in September 2015 – and which provocatively opposed not only the insurgents but also Western consensus –, also belongs here.

No matter how bold and determined President Putin is, his plans still take reality into account. Russia isn't preparing to take over the role of the hegemonic power of a unipolar world order. Neither its economic nor its military potential is sufficient for this – although there would be demand and ambition even for this – but Russia is working to restore its former superpower status and wants to resurrect the good old bipolar world. Putin doesn't hide this intention: in a memorable speech at the 2015 autumn session of the UN, praising the advantageous effect of the one-time Yalta agreement, he outlined a plan for this multipolar (in fact, bipolar) world order which he considered desirable. According to this, Russia would receive a completely free hand in its own sphere of influence, whilst its interests would also be taken into account on important strategic issues beyond its sphere of influence. It doesn't offer much in return for all this. It renounces the threat to the rest of the world, so to speak; it offers *peace in exchange for territory.*

For countries that don't fall within the supposed Russian sphere of influence, the offer may seem tempting. *Peace for territory* seems like a pretty good deal. But history teaches us (remember the failure of the pre-World War II appeasement policy, when Western powers – through constant concessions – wanted to put the brakes on Hitler, whose appetite was only increased by this) that expansionist, repressive powers only adhere to agreements as long it suits their interests and until they feel strong enough to throw off the shackles. There is no guarantee that this 'dirty bargain' will bring lasting peace to humanity. Indeed, it's more likely that such a power bargaining would increase the tyrant's appetite for further expansion.

2.) China

There's another strong challenger to the current world order: China. It, though, has chosen a different path to Russia. As a large country with several millennia of imperial past and culture, for the moment it's biding its time. It possesses a special capability that Russia and other emerging powers lack. Strategic patience. The Chinese leaders believe they have time; there's no reason to hurry. Their strategic goal will fall into their lap sooner or later. They have a strong belief that China will be the world's main economic power in the foreseeable future and, given time, can outperform all its competitors militarily (at present, not the United States, but Russia and India), meaning that it won't have to fight for hegemony as it will be its automatic right.

Although China always talks in official statements about the necessity for a new multipolar world order, and in the mid-term, this certainly is the goal, it views this only as an interim position on the road to a unipolar world position of hegemonic power. The Chinese leaders leave increasingly less doubt about their intentions. This is evidenced by President Xi-Jinping's combative speech at the Chinese Communist Party's 21st Congress in October 2017, in which he espoused the belief that by 2050, China would be the world's most significant power.

The Chinese leadership has begun its 'long march' along this path. It as a conscious step-by-step approach to military development, significantly increasing its military budget year after year. Modernisation of the navy has begun. China has already created seven artificial islands in the South China Sea, three of which already serve as naval, military, and airbases. In doing so, China has created the theoretical opportunity to close or restrict the world's busiest shipping trade route at any time.

Approximately five thousand billion dollars' worth of goods pass through this shipping route each year; the bulk of Japan's, Taiwan's, South Korea's raw material imports and finished goods exports are transported here. If China closes this shipping route, not only will these three countries find themselves in a highly critical situation and become easily blackmailed or even forced to their knees, but the entire world economy could also become mired in serious crisis.

In the current situation, of course, China can't do this, because to do so would risk U.S. military action, the consequences of which could be catastrophic, especially for China, but indeed for the whole world. China doesn't currently take this risk; it only builds up strong positions for such time when the guarantee of the current hegemonic superpower will no longer be globally valid and won't cover the whole of world trade.

3.) The pre-eminent country's worries
At the moment, neither Russia and China, individually or together, are capable of radically changing the balance of power and turning it to their advantage. At the same time, of course, both countries can cause serious disruptions to the international system, albeit at a price that puts them at least as at much risk as it does the United States and its allies. For the time being, neither their economic nor their military might is sufficient for them to carry out their ambitious plans. Although a short-term tactical alliance between them is conceivable, in the long run their interests fundamentally run into each other, so they can't form a true strategic alliance.

Now, though, they could easily get dangerously close to their coveted goal. This is due in no small part to President Obama's pacifist-, and President Trump's inconsistent, unpredictable foreign policies. President Trump's foreign policy, with its unpredictability, unexpected twists and ill-considered steps, greatly contributed to the erosion of the world order that still exists but is drifting towards crisis. It would be premature to mourn the dominant superpower status of the United States, but that this status has been shaken is obvious to everyone. All this, meanwhile, was exacerbated by the serious risks of a transactional foreign policy based on bilateralism.

The election of President Biden has significantly improved the chances of U.S. foreign policy breaking from the Jacksonian misconception and reaffirming its role as the pillar of our world order. However, after Trump's four-year cycle, it will be much harder than it was before. It probably won't be possible to return to the same place from whence Trump's presidency began.

What for us, that is, the Western world, is a risk, constitutes an opportunity for China and Russia. If the United States doesn't take on the difficult responsibility as role of guarantor of stability, that stability is unlikely to last. If NATO weakens, if the United States relativizes bilateral defence agreements (with Japan, South Korea, and Taiwan), if it sits idly by at Russia's aggression in Ukraine, or expansionism in the South China Sea, the world will become a much more treacherous place and the current world order will, in the foreseeable future, be overturned. Its rules are already disintegrating.

Hopefully none of this will come to pass, but we clearly can't rule this out today. The fate and future of the current world order depends heavily on the U.S. leadership becoming aware of the serious security risks in the world, sensing the weight of the leadership's responsibility, and being ready to take on the thankless task of being the indispensable nation in maintaining world order. Western Allies are anxiously hoping that Biden's administration will be ready and able to do so.

Why wouldn't a multipolar world be safe?

Theoretically, of course, this is also possible, and an ideal world could also rest on the constructive cooperation of several poles.

Here and now, though, there's a great danger that the multipolar world order that would most likely emerge with the current likely actors wouldn't bring lasting peace and prosperity, but rather, rivalry for power, insecurity and, ultimately, could also even lead to chaos and anarchy.

A desirable multipolar world order is based on a common set of values for the pre-eminent powers, consensual rules, and effective sanctions for breaking the rules. Surely there is little chance of this at the moment, given the possible actors. In the most likely scenario, the fragile balance of regional orders would persist for some time: an Orwellian world with three continental superpowers. It would pretty much look like everyone would be given a free hand around their own house and could practically do whatever they want within their sphere of interest. This would be the way of the strong, that is, the law of the jungle would prevail within each regional order, the victims of which would be primarily small and medium-sized nations, unable to defend their interests against the regional superpower. As long as there is a balance of power between the hegemonic powers of the poles, the oppressed, those dissatisfied with their situation, would find themselves in a hopeless position, as they wouldn't really be able to count on help from anywhere else. It would be much more a graveyard peace than a world of harmony based upon the mutual consent of the parties. It would be similar in many ways to the stability of a bipolar world, with all its injustices.

This condition, too, would only persist as long as the dissatisfied and aggrieved believe that they have more to lose through protest and rebellion than they do from acquiescence. However, if they see a chance to change the situation, then even the appearance of peace would be over. Lasting peace and stability, even at a regional level, wouldn't be guaranteed by a multipolar world order.

It's conceivable that, temporarily, the leading powers of each pole would live in peace with each other, but this would hardly be long lasting. Given that the values of the leading powers of each pole differ, their ambitions cross, and their interests may conflict, sooner or later conflict between the poles is inevitable. In academic works on this there are always responsible participants who settle their conflicts among themselves according to commonly agreed dispute settlement rules, taking into account the provisions of international law. If this were the case in reality there'd be no problem with the multipolar world. Unfortunately, the harsh reality doesn't draw on the literature. It's therefore much more likely that over time, competition could also lead to real conflict – war – between the parties. In the current situation, with the challenges we know today, more poles promise us less security and less stability than the current situation.

What would a desirable future look like?

Everyone imagines this differently, depending on their values, their interests, and their chosen strategic objectives.

We Hungarians are part of Western civilization based on the values of freedom, and it's worth thinking about a desirable future from this perspective. It would be nonsense to deny that the current world order is under strain, and that in its current form, is difficult to maintain. Moreover, it's also clear that currently, the United States is reluctant to make the sacrifices it requires to maintain this world order. If this doesn't change in the short term, the western alliance will continue to erode, and this could be fatal for the liberal world order.

It isn't yet possible today to see how the coronavirus epidemic will affect the future of a world order that's already in crisis. Some expect China's weight and influence to increase and believe the geopolitical balance will tip in China's favour. They don't see the absolute growth in China's economic and military potential as being the reason behind it, given that the epidemic has also affected China. This is shown by the fact that for the first time in thirty years, the output of the Chinese economy didn't increase, but fell in the first half of 2020. They expect China's influence to grow because the Western world has lost its self-confidence, is plagued by internal turmoil, and U.S. foreign under Trump was unpredictable and difficult to follow. Others, though, bet on Chinese influence diminishing because they believe a deglobalisation process will begin after the epidemic. Or perhaps the slowing down of globalisation (slowbalisation). This would result in supply chains being rearranged, moving closer to consumption. They believe that China will inevitably lose out in this process. Finally, we can't rule out the possibility that after the epidemic, no one will be a geopolitical winner and that all participants will be weakened, which could easily lead to the disintegration of the world order, to chaos and anarchy. There is hardly any debate as to whether this is the most alarming scenario.

Any world order, though, will only survive as long as there is a pre-eminent power which is willing to take responsibility for maintaining it, and undertaking the resultant consequences. Currently, the United States is that power, but it isn't the sole beneficiary; there are several free riders. This world order is based on the achievements of Western civilization and represents its value system. It's in the interest of all nations who enjoy the benefits of Western civilization that it survives.

To avoid misunderstanding, it should be clarified that Western civilization does not equate to the western European countries with predominantly white populations but encompasses a much wider domain. All countries that accept the principles of liberal democracy, a free market economy and free trade, belong here: Japan, India, South Korea, Taiwan and many others, too.

The burden of preserving and maintaining the world order must be shared fairly and equitably among these countries. To maintain it, the accession of any country is to be welcomed, whatever their culture, should they accept and adhere to the rules that have so far guaranteed stability and the functioning of the world economy.

Trump is undoubtedly right that the United States has borne a disproportionate burden of maintaining the international order, while not benefiting from it in proportion to its efforts. If Western leaders face the challenge of the current situation responsibly, they'll work together to come up with a fair burden-sharing proposal that'll make it possible for the United States to continue to play a prominent, but no longer exclusive role in maintaining a liberal world order.

Hopefully, such a proposal will also convince the U.S. leadership that it can't rescind its leadership role with impunity, because doing so would entail serious consequences for all participants, including the United States.

Based on its historical traditions, culture and values, Hungary is clearly part of Western civilization. The survival of the social, economic, and political system that's desirable for our country is currently ensured only by the current world order, which is currently going through a time of crisis, so it's clearly in our interest to maintain, and even strengthen it. Every foreign policy move which weakens the internal cohesion of the western alliance and strengthens its internal division, is therefore detrimental, because the beneficiaries of this are the revisionist powers and external challengers who want to force on the world an order which is alien and unfavourable to us. It follows from all this that one of the strongest premises of Hungarian foreign policy strategy is that we're interested in maintaining and strengthening the international order based upon our civilisation's values. All this, of course, depends to a small extent on Hungarian foreign policy, but it also depends to a small extent, on us.

Our neighbours and our region

"A Bad neighbourhood is an Ottoman curse", goes the Hungarian proverb. Throughout our history we've unfortunately had more than our fair share of this curse. This isn't, of course, a Hungarian peculiarity; for our region it doesn't even count as being anything special. It's therefore understandable that our immediate surroundings constitute one of the most important theatres of action when it comes to current Hungarian foreign policy. It's no coincidence that the by now classic – since replaced – foreign policy doctrine of Antall and Jeszenszky named relations with neighbouring countries as being one of the three priorities. They also recognized that neighbourly relations, as opposed to bad ones, aren't a disadvantage and an obstacle, but rather an advantage and a resource.

The traditional view is that neighbours mostly play a zero-sum game with each other. They're able to win or gain an advantage mainly at the expense of each other: if one wins in a bilateral relationship, the other necessarily loses. This was pretty much the case in historical times. Conflicts were mostly settled by war, and the losing side would pay a hefty price in terms of independence or reparations.

Today's prevailing perception is that good neighbourly relations aren't a zero-sum game, but ideally a win-win situation; i.e., a mutually beneficial cooperation that benefits both parties more than if they didn't cooperate. The inverse of this is also true, though. If they don't cooperate, and even exacerbate the existing conflicts between them, the relationship can become a lose-lose situation; i.e., they both lose.

Frosty, even hostile relations with neighbouring countries, generally – with some simplification – stem from three miscible or related causes. The most common, though by no means exclusive reason is rooted in historical grievances. The second reason stems from the present, and currently unresolved situations with regards minorities, and/or disputed territorial claims, but this reason obviously also has historical antecedents. The third reason is some form of serious conflict of economic interests between the two countries. We're in the far from lucky situation of having ample examples of all three sources of conflict in our relations with neighbouring countries.

Relations between neighbouring countries in Europe (and probably in other parts of the world) have rarely been harmonious throughout history. Frequent wars, oppression, and rivalry have often undermined good relations. There are encouraging examples of how peoples and states can overcome historical grievances and antipathies, though. The best known and most heartening is the instance of Franco-German reconciliation. Despite centuries of continuous animosity, wars, territorial gains and losses, two world wars, and often conflicting economic interests, a model process of reconciliation took place between the two peoples following World War II. Relations between the two countries were settled in a series of negotiations, set out in the 1963 Elysée Treaty. This agreement, which still forms the basis of the relationship between the two countries, was down to the strategic insight of two prominent European statesmen; French President Charles de Gaulle and German Chancellor Konrad Adenauer. The treaty laid a completely new foundation for interstate relations between the two countries, which had been ancient enemies. But perhaps even more important than this agreement is that in addition to close political cooperation, reconciliation also took place at societal level.

Today there is little trace of the former hatred, contempt, and animosity between the two peoples; instead, the relationship – even in everyday life – is characterised by mutual respect and congeniality. I've met with a Rhineland German who made no secret of the fact that he felt closer to the French or Luxembourgers than with the Bavarians or 'Ossies' (former East Germans).

Unfortunately, not all historical conflicts and animosities in Europe have been so successfully quelled.

There have also been encouraging beginnings and sympathetic endeavours in our region, too, but we can hardly talk about breakthrough success. Where we live, in the Carpathian Basin, the peoples have so far lived through many, and especially more overwhelming histories than they've been able to digest. Here, few have drawn the important lessons of history that de Gaulle and Adenauer rightly recognised; that grievance politicking doesn't solve but reproduces and amplifies grievances. The majority of the peoples of our region aren't really reconciled to themselves or their own history, let alone that of their neighbours. The processing of the past is, in most countries, still incomplete or yet to start. World War II still isn't over in the social consciousness. This is evidenced by the fierce debates still taking place to this day in Hungary about the Horthy regime and it's responsibility related to the war, in Romania, about the divisive judgement of Marshall Antonescu and the Iron Guard, in Slovakia, the role of Tiso's Nazi puppet-state, in Ukraine, the role of the Kárpáti Szics and of Bandera's Organization of Ukrainian Nationalists, and in Serbia, the hostilities between the Chetniks and Partisans. It's a similar story in Croatia when it comes to evaluating the fascist state of Ante Pavelić's Ustaša, whilst even peaceful Slovenia is extremely divided when it comes to the historical judgement of the Domobranstvo (Slovene Home Guard). Only Austria avoided these fierce debates, by sensibly presenting itself as the first victim of Nazi expansionism.

In this region, therefore, history lives with us, not in the usual sense that we know about it, and haven't forgotten it, but also in the literal sense of it being at the centre of public debate; a weapon in political discourse. If it's true that even World War II isn't over in our region, then the subsequent communist past we share with all our neighbours except Austria, is even more omnipresent, permeating everyday life.

It's important to mention all this because it also makes many things about present-day conflicts and discord understandable. The second set of sources of conflict, though, don't feed directly from the past, albeit they also have a historical background. We Hungarians also have plenty of experience when it comes to these. As a result of the unjust Trianon Peace Treaty, significant territories were annexed from Hungary and, in them, a large number of Hungarians found themselves living under the jurisdiction of neighbouring countries. More than a third of the Hungarian population at the time was stranded outside the new borders, and many completely Hungarian settlements, even completely Hungarian districts, fell under foreign rule.

This in itself sowed the seeds of later conflicts, but the real tensions arose not only from the border changes, but also from the frequent and mass violations of the rights of the Hungarian population across those borders. The Hungarian grievance politicking between the two world wars was largely fuelled by these actual violations. Of course, this also had a historical antecedent, as during the Austro-Hungarian Monarchy, minorities in Hungary experienced similar violations of the law. That is, it's a spiral of conflict, which, if not dealt with in time, can lead to a constant escalation of mutual hatred, discord and, ultimately, even armed conflict.

The injustice committed against Hungary and the violations of the rights of Hungarian nationalities, even if not justifying it, may explain Hungary viewing their role in the Second World War as being a tragic one. The two Vienna Awards, and then the Paris Peace Treaties after the war, failed to alleviate but instead intensified and fed the misery and resentment of the countries of Central Europe, including approving the total disenfranchisement and persecution of certain minorities, such as Hungarians in Slovakia or Sudeten Germans.

Everyone has their own hard-to-forget wounds and tragedies from this era. We have a hard time forgetting the deportation of Hungarians from the Felvidék (Upper Hungary), the atrocities of the Maniu Guards in Romania, and the Serbian partisans' bloodshed in Vojvodina, but the other side also mentions the atrocities of the Rongyosgárda (Ragged Guards) in Transcarpathia.

The situation of the Hungarian nationalities during the communist period didn't improve in most countries either. From this point of view, the former Yugoslavia can be considered an exception, the rights of the Hungarian nationality being widely guaranteed within the autonomy of Vojvodina. It's true that this permissive minority policy accelerated the assimilation, or at least alienation of the Hungarian nationality from the motherland and the establishment of a specific new identity; the Hungarians of Yugoslavia.

Communist Hungary didn't undertake to represent the rights of Hungarians beyond its borders. Referring to the principles of proletarian internationalism, it proclaimed that the classless society of communism provided an automatic remedy for the problems of nationality caused and, deliberately whipped up by, bourgeois nationalism and financial capitalism. This, of course, was a dogmatic lie that had nothing to do with the everyday reality of the repressive, assimilatory, 'showcase minority politics' of 'existing socialism'.

We arrived at the year of the regime change in such a way that most of the grievances hadn't been remedied, the problems only cloaked by general repression, or the communists having swept them under the rug. In the mood of clemency of the 'Year of Miracles', many of us lived in the naïve idealism that freedom would automatically solve these problems. In the days of the Romanian Revolution (the true nature of which has been much debated from the off, but I still call it this for the sake of simplicity), the oppressed, regardless of ethnicity, seemed to come together for the sacred goal of getting rid of the tyrant Ceauşescu. It's memorable that a wave of protests that united Hungarians and Romanians began around the resistance of a young Hungarian Reformed pastor in Timişoara, László Tőkés, and eventually swept away Ceauşescu's dictatorship. It's no coincidence that in the days of the revolution so many ecclesiastical and civic initiatives in Hungary, as well as many Hungarian citizens, rushed to the aid of the poverty-stricken Romanian population. At the turn of 1989-90, aid convoys continually went to Romania and Hungarians welcomed those fleeing there with great enthusiasm. Unfortunately, the state of grace and euphoria didn't last long, the anti-Hungarian atrocities of 'Black March' in Târgu Mureş in 1990 already indicating that the ethnic tensions swept under the carpet were very real and could easily take on a brutal form.

The transition to democracy in Czechoslovakia also promised that together, we'd free ourselves from the shadows of the past and the ethnic tensions that had poisoned the relationship between the two countries. Unfortunately, this also seemed like an unfounded hope. Communism didn't eradicate nationalism, only partly forced it underground and partly ensnared it in its own service (this was especially true in Ceauşescu's Romania), so after the fall of communism, when there was in any case an ideological vacuum, it became a ubiquitous and manifest political force. In the Slovak democratic opposition movement VPN (Publicity Against Violence), there was still full agreement between Slovak and Hungarian political leaders on the need for a democratic transition, respect for democratic rights and the settlement of the situation of the Hungarian minority there, but this didn't last long and after Slovakia became independent in 1993, relations between the majority and the minority became particularly strained. Slovakia's long-serving strongman Prime Minister Vladimír Mečiar played a major role in this, but the real damage was carried out by Ján Slota's SNS (Slovak National Party). A coalition of these two politicians led Slovakia between 1992 and 1998.

In Yugoslavia, the situation took a dramatic turn with the rise of Slobodan Milošević and the abolition of the autonomy of Vojvodina. The Hungarian minority, which until then had lived undisturbed and in relative peace, became targets for resurgent Serb nationalism, and was subjected to a great number of atrocities during the Yugoslav wars between 1991 and 1995, and then again during the 1999 NATO intervention in Kosovo.

Hungary's policy when it comes to neighbouring countries, which many have dubbed 'neighbourly', set itself the goal of providing a contractual basis and framework for dealing with escalating conflicts and, wherever possible, securing minority rights by way of treaty. The first such comprehensive treaty on good-neighbourly relations, modelled on the Franco-German Elysée Treaty and subsequently named the Basic Treaty for simplicity's sake, was signed by József Antall's government in December 1991 with the newly independent Ukraine. This was later followed by the Hungarian-Slovak, and then the Hungarian-Romanian Basic Treaty during the Horn government. As Secretary of State for Foreign Affairs of the then government, I myself was one of the architects of the internationally acclaimed (of course, not overly well received at home) 'good-neighbours' policy. I still take responsibility for this today, despite the partial successes and failures of Hungarian good neighbourly policy

83

When we made good neighbourly relations a priority of our foreign policy, we consciously went beyond the basic position of the previous Hungarian foreign policy and sought to find solutions to open issues and problems through the relations as a whole. We believed that good neighbourly relations have an indirect positive effect on the situation of Hungarians, and on the political climate around them. We thought that in an atmosphere of improving relationships, we could also take the initiative to remedy grievances. Our Hungarian opponents accused us of being insensitive to the problems of Hungarian minorities, sweeping violations under the carpet, and sacrificing the Hungarians minorities on the altar of good relations. Although there wasn't any truth to these accusations, they've unfortunately proved to be effective arguments in domestic policy debates that are still brought up today. In contrast, the truth is that, with the help of our policy towards neighbouring countries we made significant progress on a number of issues in the field of minority rights, and we were also able to improve the country's external image. Previously, many Western leaders had ranked us among the region's troublemakers, whilst this openly undertaken positive neighbouring country policy lifted us out of this milieu. At the same time, though, it must be objectively acknowledged that the Hungarian 'good neighbours' policy didn't fully live up to expectations.

It takes two to tango, as they say. For this policy to be truly successful, we would have needed similarly committed, compromise-seeking, and constructive partners. These, though, were in short supply in our region in the 1990s. It's indeed true that the provisions for the protection of minorities contained in the treaty were often incompletely enforced, or that the joint committees responsible for their supervision often functioned only formally, not carrying out any substantive activities. Despite all these problems I believe that it was right for us to politically promote and institutionally strengthen good neighbourly relations, because it's based on the recognition that we must live with our neighbours over the long-term. We can't replace or swap them; that is, a true resource must be created for the country out of this given situation. It would be worthwhile returning to these objectives in a renewed form, under much more favourable external conditions given that we are tied to most of our neighbours through NATO and EU membership.

The 'good neighbours' policy also has a real success story: Hungarian-Slovenian relations. It's no coincidence that former Slovenian President Milan Kučan has often said he can't imagine a better neighbour than Hungary. This statement is a testament to true strategic insight, because the primary meaning of this isn't that there's simply no better neighbour than we are, but that Slovenia, like Hungary, needs good neighbours. Slovenia, for historical reasons, is also similar to us in this, its relations with the majority of its neighbours are burdened by conflicts and unresolved issues. It needs a partner who is in part an ally, with whom it doesn't have toxic disputes in its relationship, and with whom it can be demonstrated that Slovenia is indeed capable of constructive, neighbourly relations should it find a willing partner. Hungary is the partner who can fill this role and, for similar reasons, has an interest in doing so, since we also need a prosperous conflict-free relationship with a neighbouring country. This strategic recognition slowly matured amongst the leaders shaping Hungarian foreign policy, who for a long time saw Slovenia as being our smallest and most insignificant neighbour. For a long time, I myself was not aware of the real significance of this system of relations in Hungarian foreign policy. This recognition was strengthened during my preparation for my assignment as Ambassador to Slovenia, and I already dedicated my ambassadorial work to building this strategic relationship. I often criticise the foreign policy of the current Hungarian government, so fairness demands that I acknowledge that the foreign ministers of the Orbán government and the prime minister himself deserve great credit for shaping Hungarian-Slovenian relations into strategic cooperation. The tried and tested forms of cooperation in this field can also serve as a model in other neighbourhood relations as best practice.

The third source of tension and conflict within neighbourhood relations is the serious or perceived conflict of economic interests. We also have more than one example of this. Relations with Austria were, for a long time after the change of regime, completely smooth and trouble-free. Austria is an outstanding trade and economic partner, an important investor, with high levels of reciprocal tourism, and friendly, cooperative political relations characterising this neighbourly relationship. The first more serious economic – albeit there was a political background – conflict arose between the two countries over the Nabucco pipeline. Nabucco was a plan for an alternative gas pipeline that would have delivered Central Asian and Azerbaijani gas to Europe via Turkey. Austria came up with the idea for this plan and the consortium was led by the Austrian energy giant ÖMV. Hungary were reluctant participants in the plan and actually did much to make the project impossible. Albeit it wasn't because of Hungary that the Nabucco plan failed, the Austrians also blamed us for it. This was followed by an attempt by ÖMV to acquire MOL, which Hungary considered hostile. After 2010, the Hungarian government imposed special taxes –

which were classified as being disproportionately high – on large international companies, and which especially had a detrimental effect on Austrian financial institutions. The existing economic conflicts were exacerbated by the fact that in 2018 the ÖVP-FPÖ (People's Party-Freedom Party) coalition cut family benefits for foreign workers and, in discussions on the EU's seven-year budget, also took a stance which was against Hungary's interests, advocating the redesign and reduction of subsidies and, additionally, has challenged the Commission's approval of the Paks 2 nuclear power plant before the European Court of Justice. Thus, a previously exemplary, conflict-free relationship has now become fairly tense, almost exclusively for economic reasons.

A very similar thing happened with Hungarian-Croatian relations. In the beginning, though, these had initially shown great promise. Hungary actively supported Croatia's independence aspirations from the very beginning, being among the first to recognise an independent Croatian state, and then consistently assisting during the process of joining both NATO and the EU. It was a symbolic message that one of the main objectives of the Hungarian EU Presidency was to conclude the EU-Croatia accession negotiations, which we were able to achieve on the last day of our presidency. Despite the highly favourable background, these relations have by now become quite tense and quarrelsome, the main reason for which lies in the privatisation of INA. Energy giant INA is one of the flagships of the Croatian economy. It was privatised by Hungarian company MOL and then, under disputed circumstances, taken over. The legitimacy of this is still disputed by Croatia, but it hasn't been able to prove the alleged corruption beyond reasonable doubt. Since then, all international forums have ruled that MOL's management rights over INA are legal. Many tensions have arisen. The law is in favour of MOL, but the Croatian government hasn't yet accepted this. Resolving the stalemate would be in the fundamental interest of both countries, as this conflict has already caused far more damage in international relations than the real material aspect of the disputed issue. MOL has very correctly offered to sell its stake to the Croatian government, to which they've reacted positively in principle, but to date they haven't offered an acceptable purchase price. The gravity of the conflict is well illustrated by the fact that the United States has already acted urgently to bring the matter to a fair conclusion. This example shows that even in a bilateral relationship with otherwise excellent foundations, it's easy to get into a lose-lose position even though all the conditions for a win-win situation are in place.

The most significant achievement of our regional policy is the Visegrád Group, which was also established on the initiative of Hungary in 1991 and has now become a political trademark of our region. At the time of its formation it served a dual purpose. On the one hand, it was the 'elite club' of the countries in transition, a community of leaders and, on the other, it constituted an alliance of mutual protection against the threat of Soviet intervention in the Baltics. This collaboration has a long and varied past, but its viability is proven by the fact that it exists to this day and has gained widely accepted authority for itself. It survived the Mečiar era in Slovakia and the sceptical attitude of Czech Prime Minister Klaus towards cooperation. The Visegrád Four launched the Central European Free Trade Agreement (CEFTA), which then became independent and still operates having split from the founding body (membership automatically terminates upon accession to the EU). The merit of CEFTA for many years was that the Czech Republic didn't withdraw from the cooperation. Prime Minister Klaus repeatedly said that for him this was the only tangible benefit and point of the Visegrád Four. CEFTA was, on one hand, a kind of lobby group for EU member states where participants could exercise the effects of free trade on their economies under controlled conditions, and, on the other, had a really positive effect and clearly increased intra-cooperation trade and economic relations.

EU membership has opened a new chapter in the history of the V4 countries. At the same time, it's given this form of cooperation a new role, after 2004 becoming a forum for coordinating the EU policies of the countries concerned and, where appropriate, a platform for common positions. Visegrád agreements have become regular occurrences before European summits, but the parties' viewpoints on EU issues are also continually discussed at ministerial level.

The main advantage of the V4 lies in its flexibility. To date, it has no permanent institutional bodies expect for the International Visegrad Fund. There is no pressure for the members to agree, and there's no such expectation, so consultations only take place on issues where there is a clear chance of a common position. Should they not come to an agreement, each party retains the right to represent an independent position. V4 does not have a permanent secretariat, the secretariat being provided by the country holding the presidency – which rotates on an annual basis – at the given time.

The only permanent institution is the Bratislava-based International Visegrád Fund, established in 2000, which is a donor organisation that supports initiatives to promote regional cooperation. The viability and attractiveness of the Visegrád Group is well illustrated by the fact that many countries are looking for closer cooperation with it and from time to time the issue of expanding the V4s also arises.

Although at some point, a Czech, a Hungarian and a Polish leader has raised the issue of possible enlargement (the accession of Austria, Slovenia, Croatia and the Baltic states has been mentioned several times), going by the prevailing consensus the Visegrád Group is a closed group, cannot be expanded, but on an ad-hoc basis, is open to cooperation with the countries of the region within the framework of the Visegrád+ programme. The V4 countries can already boast of many successes in this field.

The Visegrád Group is a common treasure of – and a common interest for the survival of – the four countries of the region. The countries holding similar, or the same position on the issue of immigration, appears to have strengthened the group.

There have also been worrying signs of erosion in recent years, though. Many consider the so-called Slavkov Declaration – a loose trilateral cooperation between Austria, the Czech Republic, and Slovakia – to signal the death knell of the Visegrád Group. From the moment of the Slavkov Declaration's inception it has been surrounded by the suspicion that it's some sort of rival to the Visegrád Group, a parallel framework of cooperation and, for the Czech Republic and Slovakia, could be a means of stealth distancing. These presumptions have of course been vehemently refuted by all those concerned and it's highly unlikely that this was initially really the case. The turning point by all accounts came at the extraordinary EU summit in Bratislava in September 2016. It was then that it became clear to the Czech and Slovak leadership that the Visegrád Group was no longer advantageous, but also increasingly a burden. In part, they didn't agree with the rigid anti-Brussels rhetoric and provocative actions of their Hungarian and Polish counterparts and, in part, they perceived the deteriorating prestige and toxic effect of the Group. Analysts consider the two countries efforts to break away from the Hungarian and Polish positions that hallmark the Visegrád Four countries, as starting here. This is also alluded to by the fact that several leading analysts are no longer talking of a V4, but of a V2+2.

A fault line in the debate on the future of Europe is also perceptible. Although all four countries have reservations about the model of a multispeed Europe, which is understandable given their situation, the Czech and Slovak diplomacy approach the issue in a constructive and realistic manner, in the spirit of cooperation and with far-reaching internal perspectives. Hungary and Poland are currently still in a position of rigid rejection that denies the realities. This also worsens their future negotiating positions and strengthens those efforts which aim to push these two countries to the periphery. Poland and Slovakia approve and support a reconstruction programme to address the economic effects of the coronavirus epidemic, whilst Hungary and the Czech Republic have reservations. Slovakia's new government, elected in spring 2020, as opposed to its predecessor, has a clear pro-European stance.

The Visegrád Group is currently going through a difficult period and its survival isn't automatically guaranteed. All the participants have a role to play if they want to preserve this valuable form of regional cooperation. Hungary (and, of course, the other participants as well) have a basic interest in the close cooperation of the Visegrád Four, as many important European decisions can only be influenced by joint action. Primarily, Hungary and Poland in particular need to show more flexibility because their unfavourable reputation and problems with the rule of law, in addition to their previously rigid position on immigration or the future of Europe, could be a precursor to the disintegration of internal cohesion, and the perceptible distancing of the Czechs and the Slovaks from the group.

Presently, regional relations are the neglected stepchild to the doctrine of the Eastern Opening and don't enjoy priority in the government's foreign policy   objectives. A new Hungarian foreign policy strategy must restore the balance of the main objectives, and regional policy must regain its rightful place in our foreign policy.

The new Hungarian foreign policy must come to the realisation that for economic, national strategic, and geopolitical reasons, regional policy is of paramount importance. **Hungary should pursue a constructive regional policy based on mutual respect, the promotion of common interests and the establishment of win-win cooperation with all partners who are ready to do so.** This does not in any way mean unprincipled compromises, the abandonment of interests, or the abandonment of conflict avoidance. The identified national interests must also be taken into account in regional policy, but at the same time we must refrain from stirring up self-serving conflicts and senseless arguments.

It's also important that we build a coalition in the region based on common interest, both in EU affairs and in terms of regional security and geopolitical interests, jointly managing the risks and responding to threats.

The Visegrád Group is an especially important, valuable platform for Hungarian foreign policy, and should be safeguarded. Previously, it was a pressure group which carried much weight within the EU. The noticeable weakening of the Visegrád Group is a legitimate concern. It can't be ruled out that Hungary and Poland's EU-sceptic, separate path will lead to internal uncertainty and could strengthen the Czech Republic's and Slovakia's perceptible distancing, and their efforts to loosen ties. **The new foreign policy must do everything in its power to restore the smooth running, unity, and prestige of the Visegrad Group.** It's in Hungary's basic interest to expand the scope and influence of the Visegrád Group and to establish closer relations with other Central European countries.

The European Union and Hungary within it

The European Union is currently going through an especially critical period in its turbulent history. According to common wisdom, the development of the EU has always been accompanied by crises and, so far, the EU has strengthened from all these crises and moved closer to the goals of the founding fathers. Optimists may draw strength from the fact that this has been the case thus far, but there's no guarantee that this'll be the case now. The current internal crisis in the Union seems bigger and deeper than ever.

Public opinion within, and the political elites of the European Union had previously firmly believed in the process of integration and no matter how much disagreement there was on an important, or less important secondary issue, integration itself was never questioned. The compromises necessary following heated debate may have been reached because there was a consensus that even an unfavourable compromise was a hundred times better than the dangerous alternative of disintegration. What makes the current situation dramatic is that there are more and more participants who'd vote for moving apart, separation, and disintegration rather than accepting a compromise that's less favourable to them.

Brexit is an important turning point in this process. Until 2016, the history of the European Union, as well as its predecessor organisations, took place under the spirit of continuous expansion. Thus, the founding six became nine in 1973, twelve by 1986, fifteen in 1995, twenty-five during the historic enlargement to the east in 2004, twenty-seven in 2007, and finally twenty-eight in 2013. Another five countries are currently waiting in line as candidates for membership, and then there are more potential candidates.

One of the most important proofs of the EU's success has been that it has been an attractive and desirable goal for non-members until recently, and that those inside have been proud of their membership. Continuous enlargement isn't only tangible evidence of success, but the essence of how the Union works. There are those who liken the working principle of the Union to that of a bicycle: if we don't pedal, we'll fall. History also knows many examples of when the expansion of an empire stops it's a sure sign of the impending failure of the empire and, a precursor to disintegration.

The only minor disturbing episode in this long success story was the 1985 Greenland split, but seeing as it wasn't a whole country but a province that withdrew from European cooperation here, with very little economic impact for the EU as a whole, it had no effect on the prestige of enlargement policy. The situation is quite different with the exit of the United Kingdom. This is both a consequence but also a further trigger for the EU's internal crisis.

In Britain, the 2016 referendum on membership, via which they ultimately decided to leave, took place at the height of a protracted period of crisis. Although the global financial crisis that began in 2008 started in America and initially affected them the most, it hit Europe much longer and deeper. While the recession in the United States was relatively short (two to three years) and followed by a period of strong growth, the European crisis dragged on, pushing some countries close to bankruptcy (including Hungary, Ireland, Portugal and, most importantly Greece), and in 2011-2012 a second wave of recession also emerged, this protracted period of crisis only came to a clear end in 2016. However, this was by no means the only crisis that the EU has had to deal with during this period.

The Arab Spring initially filled European leaders with the hope that a democratic transformation would begin everywhere in the Mediterranean basin. The encouraging processes unfortunately turned unfavourable almost everywhere fairly quickly, and instead of the hoped-for stabilisation and consolidated liberal democracies, chaos in some countries (Libya, Yemen), another dictatorship (Egypt) and a bloody civil war (Syria) followed. The Arab Spring – with the partial and relative exception of Tunisia – hasn't yielded any real success stories anywhere. Moreover, in a confusing situation, a Sunni terrorist organization called Islamic State was formed, and which with dizzying speed and surprise spread its control over significant areas in Iraq and Syria. In a short time, Islamic State has replaced the terrorist organisation Al Qaeda and has threatened not only the Arabian Peninsula and the stability of North Africa, but since 2015 has declared the territory of the EU to be a battleground, and its 'fighters' have carried out a series of murderous terrorist attacks in major European cities. In doing so, they've successfully undermined the sense of security of European citizens who've faced the depressing experience that, overnight, their peaceful lives have been threatened and they themselves have become the targets of terrorist attacks. Feelings of helplessness and general anxiety turned against the political elite and, within that, EU leaders. Despair convinced many that European leaders had made them vulnerable with their policies, and that they were unable or unwilling to protect ordinary citizens.

All this coincided with the immigration crisis of 2015-16, which wasn't independent of the Arab Spring, and even less of the civil wars in Iraq and Syria. In the two years of the immigration crisis almost two million asylum seekers crossed the Union's borders, and the vast majority of them went to Germany, Sweden, and Austria as destinations, but many also went to France and Great Britain, and some reached other countries. Compared to the usual maximum of two to three hundred thousand refugees in previous years, this influx put the capacity of both EU and national institutions to the test, and these institutions failed. The EU's asylum system wasn't prepared for such a mass influx, and existing regulations such as the Dublin Regulation or the Schengen Agreement have proved completely unsuitable for tackling the problem. European citizens felt that both the European Union and their own governments were powerless, devoid of a plan, and unable to keep control over the process. They felt that those whose primary responsibility was to ensure security and the smooth running of everyday life, had declared bankruptcy and betrayed them.

This influx of immigrants has also brought to the surface the complete unpreparedness, and capacity problems of the asylum system. The problem has been made particularly difficult by the fundamentally different attitudes of individual member states towards the issue of asylum seekers. Whilst most of the new member states, led by Hungary, sharply rejected the admission of asylum seekers, some member states promoted and practiced the generous *Willkommenskultur*, a culture of open arms, whereas others remained indifferent because they weren't affected by the wave of asylum seekers. Due to differing interests, different approaches and different levels of involvement, the EU has long been unable to reach a unified position on the issue and there's still no consensus on how to address the issue in the long term. The immigration crisis has created tensions both within and between many member states, causing a serious break in solidarity and internal cohesion and also raising the risk of the EU falling apart.

The EU-Turkey deal in 2016 was reached almost at the very last minute and curbed the flood – and thus the fatal deepening of the EU refugee crisis – in time. The consequence of the deal is that this issue is no longer the most urgent item on the agenda for EU leaders, but it's far from being off the agenda and so far, there's no reassuring solution.

Tensions caused by the refugee crisis have eased, but in parallel, other crises have continued to adversely affected the European mood. Among these, one that stands out is the challenge that Russia poses to European countries through its expansionist endeavours and efforts to gain influence. Although this didn't begin in 2014, it was then that it became apparent and threatening to Europe. It was during 2014 that Russia occupied and then annexed Crimea following a referendum of dubious legitimacy, and since then has effectively been waging a proxy war in Eastern Ukraine by providing open military support for the separatist forces. In so doing, it not only violated its former contractual obligations, but also one of the basic principles of the international order; the inviolability of borders and respect for territorial integrity. In the same year, a large-scale so-called hybrid war against several EU member states began. Within the framework of hybrid warfare, Russian secret services engage in a wide range of disinformation activities, spread false news, create confusion, obtain and use sensitive data through cyber warfare, support extremist parties and movements, influence elections and, in some cases (Montenegro), support coup attempts. This is complemented by diplomatic efforts. They seek to divide the EU and NATO, to dismantle the unity of the EU through member states that are willing to do their bidding, and they assert their own interests through the leaders of certain member states.

Trouble never comes alone. In Turkey, meanwhile, which has been an EU candidate since 1999, things took a turn for the worse in 2016 with an aborted coup attempt. President Erdoğan embarked on a brutal cleansing operation that resulted in hundreds of thousands losing their jobs, more than a hundred thousand people, including teachers, judges, journalists, police and military officers interned, and many convicted. Press freedom has been all but abolished in Turkey, human rights are constantly being seriously violated, and even the pretence of the rule of law is no longer maintained. Understandably, accession negotiations with the country have also stalled, but now Erdoğan is also bragging that Turkey doesn't even need EU membership. That is, this once-promising accession process is now in a hopeless situation, and Turkey is no longer a predictable, friendly partner.

Brexit, though, has more serious consequences for the EU than all the crises listed so far. The British decision to leave was certainly influenced by the series of crises and the EU's wavering, procrastination, and debatable responses to it, but the real reason for leaving is a deep crisis that affects not only the EU, but all the democracies of Western liberalism. This is the creeping crisis of the socio-economic-political model of the Western world which became apparent following the global financial crisis. In short, we could say that the previous consensus has crumbled, and public confidence in the elite, in the political system and, in the economic institutions of the system, has been shaken. The former firm belief in the moral supremacy and omnipotence of liberal democracy and a market economy based on liberal principles has disintegrated, and the vacuum created in its place has been partly filled by frustration, indifference and disillusionment, whilst left- and right-wing populism, protest parties, as well as anti-elite and anti-globalisation forces endeavour to fill the gap. The process didn't begin in 2008, although the financial crisis did give it much impetus. It certainly started around the turn of the millennium, and if not spectacularly, the forces that the previous consensus faced grew stronger year by year. The common feature of this very heterogeneous society, both ideologically and organisationally, is Euroscepticism or even open anti-Europe sentiment.

For a long time, this phenomenon wasn't given real attention by members of the traditional elite because it wasn't really perceptible to the naked eye, but now some form of populism exists in most countries of the continent, has strong support in many of them, a strong parliamentary presence, and has already reached governmental power in a few countries. Brexit is also part of this process; one of its most spectacular symbols. It's true that the expected big populist breakthrough in 2017 didn't take place in France, the Netherlands or Germany, but in all these countries, extremism also strengthened significantly and took on a role that seriously influenced the European political climate. In the Italian parliamentary elections of March 2018, anti-elite, partly extremist forces won more than fifty percent of the vote. The 2019 European elections didn't bring a breakthrough for extremist forces, but they were undoubtedly able to strengthen their political representation. The proportion of populist, extremist and Eurosceptic MEPs in the EP rose from 24% to 29%.

The problem is exacerbated by the fact that the trend in populism in the new member states is particularly strong and, in many cases, has already risen to the level of government policy. Among these, Hungary, whose government led by Viktor Orbán has been a pioneer in the process since 2010, stands out. It was joined by the Polish government led by PiS in 2015, and which was re-elected in 2019, but there was also a tendency in the Slovak governments of Robert Fico from 2006 to 2019, during the time of Bulgarian Prime Minister Boyko Borisov or Traian Băsescu in Romania, and similar fears have been expressed following the election victory of Czech politician Andrei Babiš. The Hungarian and Polish examples, however, stand out from the populisms of the other new member states because their profile expressly includes Euroscepticism, sometimes open anti-Europeanism in the shape of the 'war of independence' against

Brussels. Both are in constant dispute with the European mainstream, consciously provoking internal discord, spectacularly confronting European values and also creating a platform, a 'counter-model' based on purely governmental cooperation, which it calls 'Europe of the Nations'.

The traditional European elite is seemingly helpless in the face of the rise of populism and unable to halt the process of internal erosion. The debate on the Future of Europe which began and then was postponed, and which may be resumed in autumn 2020, will only have sense if the process of European unity has an encouraging perspective, and a real future. This issue hasn't yet been decided definitively. It all depends on who's able to give more faith and hope to European citizens. The constructive, pro-European forces? Or will they give way to the destructive forces; the populist sharks who peddle fear and nationalism?

The stakes are high. The survival of the European integration process, and a common Europe, depend on it. One thing's for sure; inactivity or stagnation aren't a viable option. Without comprehensive reform, without innovation and a vision that inspires citizens, it's quite possible that the centuries-old dream of a united Europe will be thwarted for many years to come. Everyone is more or less aware of this. Without substantial change, the process of European integration could fail completely. Countless plans, ideas, and proposals are currently on the negotiating table. The continuum of reform ideas is wide-ranging. At one end of the spectrum comes Brexit; that is, exiting the EU, disintegration. At the other, comes a federal Europe, a United States of Europe. Of the many possibly scenarios, following the UK's departure neither of the two extreme cases are likely to materialise, but no one knows exactly what will come to pass, and whether there'll be a big compromise between the quarrelling partners or not.

As I write these lines, the Grand Plan for the future of Europe, which lacks consensus or broad support, hasn't yet been outlined. It has recently been pushed into the background, but the scenario referred to as the Macron-Merkel plan is still on the negotiating table. This scenario presupposes that there is no optimal common solution acceptable to all member states, so Europe must continue at different speeds, but chiefly at two speeds. More developed member states with an interest in deeper integration and who show constructive behaviour, for the most part, but not exclusively within the Eurozone, should establish closer cooperation, whilst the others can move more slowly, at a pace of their choice, forming a kind of periphery around the developed centre. According to Macron's ambitious, but not particularly realistic plans, this inner core is clearly also separated from the others at the institutional level. It has an independent budget, a finance minister, an established fiscal union, a separate parliament, a common army. This spectacular form of segregation, though, is opposed by the Germans, and their interests run counter to it as the new member states are an important market and expansion area for the German economy. Macron's definitive notions of an institutionally divided union are therefore likely to be much diluted during implementation, should this at all happen. A spectacular split is therefore unlikely, but the soft form of separation could easily materialise.

Although according to the Merkel-Macron plan, a couple of the new member states could join this core, the original idea could be the re-emergence of a light version of the EU before enlargement to the east. Subsequent accession to those now at the forefront wouldn't be ruled out in principle, but in practice this would become increasingly difficult as EU action in this form would strengthen divergence, not convergence. As a result of a two-speed Europe, over time, the gap may widen to the point where no one can surmount it, especially if on the other side there isn't any real readiness to receive. Brexit also sets a dangerous precedent in this context. More and more people are recommending to Eastern and Central European member states, especially to Poland and Hungary, the model they are now developing for a Britain which is leaving the Union. This would no longer be a case of cooperation on the periphery, but cooperation outside the Union.

It's not my intention to cause panic, nor do I believe that these plans can materialise in this extreme and particularly dangerous form for us, but I don't dare to rule out the possibility. For the first time in the history of the European Union, the possibility of a split in some form has arisen seriously, and not just on the drawing board.

This plan isn't only unacceptable because it's particularly detrimental to the countries that may be on the periphery, Hungary included. As a staunch Pro-European, I believe that this rift could easily even spell the end of the whole process of European integration. If the separation begins it could easily be tantamount to a death sentence for a united Europe. In the present world, though, struggling with the scourge of crises and challenges, it could spell the end not only of a noble idealistic idea, but also of our peaceful, homely world and our chosen sociopolitical economic model. In the short term, the countries of the periphery will be adversely affected, but in the long-run the continent as a whole will suffer. Disintegration may accelerate, balance of power politics may return alon with its dangerous conflicts and methods of conflict management, and everything may be buried by the threatening challenges, about which much has been said in this book.

The fact that not only President Macron and Chancellor Merkel, but many others in the western part of the Union are amenable to such plans, is in no small part down to the – to put it mildly – mixed experiences of Eastern enlargement. Thus, if we want to avoid a two-speed Europe, we also have work to do. If it's true that the danger of this happening is partly due to the processes in our region as well as down to the behaviour of some member states, then we also have a task and a role in forming a response.

The coronavirus epidemic, as well as the premonitory signs of a new Cold War, could overwrite many earlier plans. These have awoken Europe to its problems of internal division, its vulnerability and its defencelessness. The EU financial recovery fund, more important than all before it, the regulatory protection of strategic sectors against hostile buyouts by foreign third parties, as well as the buyout of the technology sectors, President Macron's initiative to create 'strategic autonomy' is an encouraging sign when looking at the promise of a new, common European future. For the time being though, we can't yet see whether the balance of power in Europe will tilt on favour of the cohesive or destructive forces.

Hungary and the EU

The change of regime offered a new chance for Hungarians to make irreversible their thousand-year dream of belonging to the West, following several unsuccessful intermissions. If there was something that the vast majority of Hungarians undoubtedly agreed with then, it was the intention to join the community of Western countries. This desire appears everywhere in the most important documents of the time. In addition to the mention of the 'Road to Damascus', this was the other most popular topic in the press at the time. It's no coincidence that Péter Esterházy wanted to financially fine those who 'take Europe in vain'; that is, who spout of about it for no reason. The material expression of this desire was the intention to join the European Community, later known as the European Union. In a statement, Prime Minister József Antall even considered it conceivable that Hungary's accession to the European Community could precede the accession of Austria. The first, perhaps most important element of the three-pronged foreign policy system he formulated, and which was in force until 2010, was precisely Euro-Atlantic accession.

In 1989, the first European aid programme to make aid available to two former communist countries was launched: the so-called PHARE program, the first two letters of which referred to the beneficiary countries, Poland and Hungary. In 1991, Hungary signed the Association Agreement, which was the first comprehensive agreement with a European partner. It's no coincidence that Hungary was the first country in the region to apply for EU membership in the spring of 1994. In 1997, the EU decided to open accession negotiations with the countries selected in the first round, the so-called Luxembourg Six, Hungary included. The accession treaty was signed by Prime Minister Péter Medgyessy in April 2003 and was confirmed by an 84% yes vote in a referendum that month, and finally on 1 May 2004, Hungary became a full member of the European Union. The fact that the turnout fell short of 50% casts a slight shadow on the impressive referendum support for accession, which could even be explained by the fact that public opinion already considered it to be a 'done deal' and didn't consider participation to be important. It could also be explained, though, by the fact that the great enthusiasm had already waned, and its place taken, in part by apathy and in part by disinterest. Close on a half of Hungarian society rather acquiesced to, but didn't have a strong identification, much less enthusiasm, for membership. The low turnout was certainly a warning sign.

2010 also sets a clear demarcation in Hungary's operation as a member state. Up until then, Hungary's European policy was explicitly one of imitation and adaptation, largely taking into account the position of the dominant member states. Critics interpreted this as meaning that the Hungarian government was pursuing a subservient European policy, playing teacher's pet at the expense of its own interests. Opposition politicians strongly rebuked former Foreign Minister László Kovács, later a European Commissioner, for one of his speeches, claiming that the basic position of the government was to 'Dare to be small!'. The then opposition, today's government, contrasted this with a 'Dare to be big!' attitude. The essence of this being that we must represent our position strongly and decisively, subordinating everything to our own interests. We see every situation as a win-lose situation, and we don't think in terms of seeking win-win situations. Despite the fact that in the first period the Hungarian attitude was basically constructive and open to compromise, it can't be considered a wholesale success. This, though, isn't primarily due to the external presentation of the policy, but to the deteriorating economic performance in the background. Although Péter Medgyessy announced his intention to join the Eurozone as soon as possible, the government's economic policy, and the performance of the Hungarian economy, pushed the country further and further from this goal. From the moment of our accession, an excessive deficit procedure was initiated against us, which only ended in 2013. The Hungarian convergence plan, that is, a credible programme for economic catch-up, wasn't accepted by the Commission for many years, because it wasn't found to be realistic or well-founded. Our data was also subjected to much criticism, this being fully confirmed by Prime Minister Ferenc Gyurcsány's speech in Öszöd, which can also be considered as a statement of admission. All this caused considerable domestic political tension and Hungary lost its internal stability after 2006. The government blocked the Nabucco project, which still enjoyed the backing of the EU, and apparently took a separate path in terms of judgement and support of the Orange Revolution in Ukraine. Hungary was also the first serious victim of the 2008 financial crisis in the EU. Only the joint loan program of the IMF and the EU saved the country from bankruptcy. After this, Hungary was increasingly seen as the 'sick man' of the EU.

Our report card from the first period of our membership is therefore mixed. The Hungarian government's behaviour, willingness to cooperate, and commitment to European values were generally assessed positively, whilst the country's vulnerability, deteriorating economic performance and, later, domestic political destabilisation, were assessed very negatively.

European partners therefore initially welcomed the change of government and attitudes in 2010 with expressly positive expectations and few shedding a tear for the ambiguous practices of previous years. Disappointment wasn't long in coming. 2010 didn't bring the necessary correction, but a radical break with previous practice. The energetic measures of the activist-minded Orbán government quickly blighted the positive expectations. With Prime Minister Orbán unable to negotiate with then Commission president Barroso to allow an increase in the budget deficit, he resorted to strong arm tactics. He imposed a multitude of special taxes on financial institutions, the energy sector, telecommunications companies, and retail chains. It wasn't so much the imposition of the special taxes, but their excessiveness and the way they were introduced, that were criticised. They were introduced almost summarily by the government, without any kind of prior consultation or preparation time. Summary legislation didn't only cover economic life. The transformation of the state system also proceeded at break-neck pace, all of this in total disregard for the principles of the rule of law, and often in clear contravention of it. Among the many controversial pieces of legislation were the radical amendment of the Constitutional Court Act, the media law, the adoption of the new single-party

Basic Law, the adoption of the electoral law, new judicial laws, and the legal transformation of the National Bank.

European governments had practically no time in which to come to their senses, and by now had to negotiate with a completely different Hungary than the one that joined the Union.

Amidst increasingly sharp and heated debates between Hungary and the EU as well as individual member states, Prime Minister Viktor Orbán declared a 'war of independence' against Brussels. The formula is simple. Brussels is the new colonial power which wants to have a say in everything, threatens our independence, and wants to tell us how to live. The government is protecting the freedom and independence of Hungarians, and its disputes with Brussels aren't about individual matters; these are a pretence, what Brussels really wants is full power, and the only problem with the Hungarian government is that it stands in the way of this endeavour. As transparent and untrue as this rhetoric was, it was surprisingly successful in the domestic political arena, making the Hungarian government's 'freedom struggle' understandable and sympathetic for many.

In 2014, the time came for this confrontation to become the dominant ideology of the state reasoning. It was then that Viktor Orbán announced the construction of the illiberal state in his speech at Băile Tuşnad. The policy of Eastern Opening is the tool to put this ideology into practice. The natural consequence of this is the 'peacock dance'; the Hungarian special path when we no longer consider the common foreign policy to be authoritative, but rather the precarious balance between East and West, not hiding that the government's more sympathetic partners are in the East. Although the cautious putting out of feelers towards the East began after 2010, it became the main focus only in the second term of government. Eastern tyrannies, autocratic states, and sometimes dictatorships, became key partners. Viktor Orbán called Russia, China, and Turkey the Holy Trinity of illiberal states, the prime examples to follow. He maintains a particularly close friendship with all three countries and is willing to pay for this even through huge investment projects (Paks 2, the Budapest-Belgrade railway line) that are especially detrimental to us.

From the very beginning, he took a position on the refugee issue that was aloof, and in practice he represented it in a ruthless manner often bordering on the inhumane, even transforming it all into a hate campaign against Brussels. With this, Hungary has taken on a new position in Europe. We were the first – by now, far from the only – to have a government that's openly against receiving refugees, and expressly hostile towards them. In doing so, the Hungarian government became the first from among the Visegrád countries, and a kind of point of reference for the European far right.

Whilst the previous Hungarian European policy could perhaps be rightly criticised for its pliancy and excessive willingness to adapt, our EU policy after 2010 is the exact opposite. The Hungarian government is seen by many as a troublemaker which disregards European values and the rule of law and betrays the common European interest; a Trojan horse with dangerous external interests, a supporter of extremism and populism, a destroyer of a harmonious, constructive, and consensus-based political culture. The former teacher's pet became the bad boy in the class.

The true danger of this precarious status could be realised in these difficult times. I've already talked about the fact that one of the most serious risks in the future of the EU is fragmentation. This danger is nurtured and reinforced to a large extent by the attitude that Hungary and Poland currently show within the European Union. Through continuous confrontation and obstruction, Hungary may marginalise itself, significantly limiting the benefits it enjoys from integration.

If these two countries don't desist with their destructive behaviour which hinders joint decisions, or if they continues to erode European values (solidarity, cohesion, and constructiveness), the process of divergence will probably be unavoidable. The primary losers in this will be those who miss out on deeper integration, but in the long run, the whole integration process and within it, the states of the centre, will also be losers.

Hungary has asymmetric capabilities when it comes to shaping the future of the EU. With constructive, and cooperative behaviour, it can but – commensurate with its size, political and economic weight – contribute to promoting positive change. This should not be under- or overestimated. We're a medium-sized member state, one out of the current 27. On the other hand, Hungary can influence the deepening of an existing crisis, the escalation of an internal conflict, to a much greater extent than its size and weight. This ability far exceeds the level of its constructive abilities. This feature is not unique to Hungary. It's also true for other member states. Think of the role of Greece in the financial crisis. It's clear that Greece had a very limited ability, or contribution to overcoming the 2008 financial crisis in Europe, but it already played a much more significant role in the deepening of the Eurozone crisis, and almost brought about the very collapse of the Eurozone.

With just a few simple steps, Hungary could greatly improve its own chances and, to a lesser extent, the chances of Europe as a whole. There are two such issues. The refugee issue, and reform of the Eurozone. By giving up its harsh, destructive behaviour on the refugee issue and the rejecting any common solution, it can help in adopting a common European asylum policy that it finds acceptable. Presently, this is one of the main fracture lines between Hungary and the leading countries of the EU. Now that Europe's energy is being spent in dealing with so many other crises, a smart compromise could be reached on good terms, and we could cast off the role of being the destroyer of unity.

The other substantive issue is the reform of the eurozone. This wouldn't appear to affect us, as we aren't members of the Eurozone and our government is suggesting that we won't be so for the foreseeable future. But this is no longer an exclusive, or even primarily a financial or economic issue, but rather, a strategic decision. If the Eurozone becomes the centre of the new Europe, for which there is every chance after the adoption of comprehensive reforms, the countries that are left behind won't only miss out on the common currency, but also the common future of Europe. What's at stake would appear to have also already been recognised in the once stubbornly non-committal Czech Republic, which has made demands for an observer membership (although one currently doesn't exist). Bulgaria and Croatia have already announced their intention to join, and both stand the chance of entering the Eurozone waiting room; that is, joining the ERM 2 mechanism. Romania is also already considering entering, although the European Central Bank's spring 2020 report states that the country doesn't yet meet any of the four accession criteria.

If Hungary doesn't want to be shunted out to the periphery, it must immediately take the first steps in this direction. This, in itself, has far-reaching implications as it isn't only a tool to help us catch up, but also a strong symbol of our commitment to an integrated Europe.

It'll be difficult to change the unfavourable image that has developed of Hungary's European commitment, and perception of the country, in one fell swoop. This is a long process that can only be started with strong impulses. Words alone no longer help. Actions are required to support the credibility of the intention to change.

It's time to end the meaningless freedom struggle against the EU. Allow me to refer to a distant historical analogy. The country was bled dry in the Rákóczi Wars of Independence, the peace of Satu Mare was required for the starting of a consolidated nation-building upon the destruction and ruins of conquest and years of war. This is what's needed today. We should make peace with those with whom we in any case share our values and interests. All the more so because in the current times of crisis, it's especially difficult to find a good reason for the current belligerence, justified by the country's interests.

The United States of America and Hungary

Until recently, the United States held the honorary title of leader of the free world. Its robust economic performance, outstanding military capabilities and commitment to leadership have made its entitlement to the title undisputable. It earned all this after World War II, when it was tasked with the difficult responsibility of defending the Western world. During the Cold War, the United States was the main guarantor of the survival of the Western world and values. When the flood of communism seemed unstoppable and its ultimate victory only a matter of time, the United States-led alliance halted the triumphal procession and curbed communist expansion. Victory in the Cold War can be attributed to several factors, but one of these is undeniably the persistent and stubborn opposition of the United States to communism, including President Reagan's at the time much-criticised Strategic Defense Initiative, or his categorical rejection of the 'Evil Empire'.

After the end of the Cold War, a new, no less serious challenge awaited the winner: the role of upholder of the unipolar world order which many call the liberal world order. The former bipolar world order was based on a balance of power between the two superpowers, with shared responsibility for stability. The unipolar world order has only one hegemonic power; it practically has sole responsibility for maintaining stability and smooth operation of the order. It has even been called the 'lone sheriff' in professional literature, and latterly, the 'reluctant sheriff'.

This role comes with a high cost, is unpopular, and entails many sacrifices, so the American public, which supported or at least accepted the former role as the defender of freedom against tyranny, isn't particularly enthusiastic about the new role.

Although at the end of the Cold War many hoped that 'history was at an end' and that serious cataclysms and conflicts were no longer expected for humanity, life very quickly dashed that hope. With the end of the Cold War the world became not more peaceful, but in a sense more dangerous and full of conflict than it was before. Whilst the two superpowers more or less kept order; that is, maintained stability in their own sphere of influence, in the new world order this kind of close supervision ceased, and many previously repressed conflicts escaped from the bottle. A good example of this is the Yugoslav crisis. In a bipolar world, the external threat held the country together but when it ceased, the repressed internal conflicts surfaced and culminated in a bloody civil war.

Up until World War II, American foreign policy alternated between inward-looking, aloof, periods of isolationism and periods of interventionism and internationalism linked with active participation. The Cold War years didn't permit the luxury of turning inward, because communist danger was a constant and immediate threat. With the end of the external existential threat, isolationism became a relevant political factor again, although until recently the administration didn't embrace it. Already when President Clinton was elected, many in the internationalist camp worried that U.S. foreign policy would turn inward because foreign policy played only a secondary role in Clinton's first presidential election campaign. This didn't materialise though, the United States eventually taking on the role bestowed upon it in the unipolar world. President Bush pursued an explicitly active foreign policy and followed interventionist traditions. His foreign policy has rightly been widely criticised for often leading recklessly, without questioning its alliances, in contravention of certain rules of international law and on the basis of unilateralism, but left no doubt that the United States is a global power which is prepared to act, and one which isn't advisable to disregard. His successor represented a completely different approach to foreign policy. Although Obama, and in particular his first Secretary of State, Hillary Clinton, wasn't isolationist, his foreign policy was decidedly low-profile, playing a secondary, subordinate role in his presidential objectives and throughout his administration. Obama's presidency had its respectable results, but foreign policy wasn't one of them. It was during this period that Russia became the main challenger to the status quo through its annexation of Crimea, China embarked upon a spectacular rearmament programme and the building of military bases on artificial islands in the South China Sea, and then, the Arab Spring was in full flow, initially an encouraging and heartening process with all its contradictions, later a huge failure democratic transition. The Syrian civil war also escalated at this time, and it was during this period that Islamic State became a serious factor in the region and Russia re-emerged as a player in the Middle East. Within a few years of Obama's presidency, a complex world situation fraught with previously unknown dangers emerged; one that would have been unimaginable a decade ago.

In this new situation, emerging revisionist powers Russia and China have already openly questioned the existing world order and the hegemonic role of the United States within it. The Western world came face to face with new, dangerous challenges exactly when it needed the leadership of the United States more than ever. From the growing military threat to climate change, from mass migration to international terrorism, from the spread of populism to the unstable world economy, to the unpredictable economic impact of the coronavirus epidemic, more and more crises have tested the Western world's resilience and ability to adapt. The world was waiting for the absent hero who would bring order in times of crisis, and the United States, which has the largest economy and the strongest military potential, would be best suited for this role. The election of President Trump completely shattered these expectations.

The messages of Trump's election campaign in 2016 caused serious alarm among U.S. allies. He called NATO obsolete, made the application of Article 5 of the Washington Treaty, which forms the basis of collective defence, conditional, relativized the content of bilateral defence treaties, threatened China with a trade war, rejected the free trade agreement for the establishment of a single transatlantic economic area (TTIP), terminated the Trans-Pacific Partnership (TPP), and raised the prospect of terminating the NAFTA agreement (although NAFTA was later renewed with another agreement). All this was crowned by the emphasis on the 'America first' principle, as well as announcing an egotistic, transactional foreign policy turn. No wonder, then, that an icy horror prevailed in the western world following Trump's election. These early concerns resolved only slowly, and only to a small extent, whilst new ones were added aplenty.

Today, we can see that what was said in the campaign was fortunately primarily for local consumption and has only been partially followed by U.S. foreign policy. In some cases the opposite has been spectacularly confirmed: for example, commitment to NATO, Article 5, and the validity of bilateral military agreements in Asia. American foreign policy, though, is characterised by a hard-to-follow detours during the Trump administration. Trump was incomprehensibly friendly towards North Korean leader Kim Jong-un, then threatened him with war, sought agreement and confrontation with the Chinese leadership, unilaterally withdrew from the Iranian nuclear deal, threatened to withdraw from the START agreement, unilaterally withdrew from the Open Skies treaty, withdrew a quarter of U.S. troops from Germany, and threatened to leave the WHO at the time of the epidemic, and so on. All of these steps have greatly contributed to the erosion of the Western alliance system and provided an impetus for the formulation of President Macron's plan for European strategic autonomy. The situation is far from reassuring.

However, Trump's presidency also had two tangible positive effects on his allies. On the one hand, he became aware that China was the number one – and real – challenger to the world order. He pointed out that China, as an economic freerider, has become the true beneficiary of globalisation. If we don't modify the boundaries of our relations with China the western world will, in the foreseeable future, become vulnerable, and this will help facilitate China gain a hegemonic position in a new world order.

As a second positive, it has helped partners recognise that the security policy's 'stray strategy' is over, and that they too need to play a greater role in maintaining a world order that benefits them and guarantees security. It would appear that many partners quickly understood its pertinence. This is evidenced by Germany and France calling for the strengthening of European defence capabilities and beginning preparations for the establishment of a future common European army. The first encouraging steps in this direction had already been taken barely a year after Trump took office. Unfortunately, though, positive action can also have negative consequences if it contributes to weakening the United States' commitment to its partners, as well as the erosion of NATO. We can but hope that the latter doesn't come to pass.

Other NATO members have also accelerated the increase in defence spending to 2% of national income. These are still primarily promises but maybe now there will also be a chance of fulfilling them. During the Cold War, the average defence spending of the then NATO member states reached 3% of national income, later falling drastically in most countries except the United States, and in 2019 only nine member states still met the criteria of 2 %, suggested at the 2014 NATO summit in Wales and which was made binding on all member states at the Warsaw summit in 2016, with a 2024 deadline. Undoubtedly, the strongest impetus to deliver on the issue of joint commitment was President Trump's rather crude intervention at the 2017 NATO summit in Brussels to increase spending.

It's undeniable that thus far, the United States has borne a disproportionate share of the high cost of world security and stability. Roughly 60% of NATO member states' total defence spending has so far been covered by the United States, one and a half times the combined contribution of other member states. Increasing military spending isn't only important for the NATO members because we really do live in a more dangerous world today than we did ten years ago and can only protect our security with greater effort, but also so they have greater autonomy in security policy and aren't vulnerable or subordinate, but true equal partners of the United States. Should this happen, Trump will undoubtedly have played an important role, however grudgingly.

European allies welcomed Biden's election with undisguised joy and considerable optimism. It's hoped that Biden will heal the wounds inflicted on the souls of America's European allies by his predecessor, and reaffirm the United States' clear commitment to NATO, in particular Article 5 of the Washington Treaty. The rekindling of this alliance is badly needed by both parties.

Hungarian-American relations

The United States is of great importance when it comes to Hungarian foreign policy strategy. NATO – the leading power of which is the United States – is the main guarantee of our securi-

117

ty. In international affairs, close cooperation can boost our ability to assert our interests, whilst deteriorating relations weaken it. It's no coincidence that most countries seek good relations and close cooperation with the United States. Anyone who has already spoken as an official representative in the decision-making centres in Washington, the White House, the NSC, the State Department, or Congress may have sensed that various international delegations are virtually tripping over each other in order to gain the goodwill and support of the hosts. I really did often have the feeling during my official visits to Washington that the city has become the new Rome; to where all roads lead, and where the most important decisions are made. Additionally, the United States is also an important partner for Hungary from an economic perspective given that it's one of the most important non-EU trading partners and also plays an important role in domestic investments. Since the change of regime, every Hungarian government has tried to build and maintain good relations, but not all of them have been successful in this, something that's especially true in recent years.

Our bilateral relations didn't develop too promisingly in the first half of the twentieth century. In World War I, as part of the Austro-Hungarian Monarchy, we were at war with the United States from 1917 onwards, making peace only in 1921 (in other words, a good while after the Trianon Peace Treaty), and establishing diplomatic relations with them only in 1922. In December 1941, under deeply strange circumstances, we were informed that we considered ourselves to be at war, which the Americans didn't understand or acknowledge at the time, it only being a year later that a state of war between the two countries was officially declared. Peace came within the framework of the Paris Peace Treaty in 1947, Hungary's image in Washington not being the best for quite some time. We were branded as a country always on the wrong side; as Hitler's last henchmen, and as Stalin's most faithful disciples. The 1956 revolution changed this in one fell swoop, radically altering the American public's and politicians' view. From then on, Hungarians became a sympathetic, freedom-loving, brave nation suffering under the yoke of communism. We got off to a great start in the years of regime change, by which time Washington already saw the Hungarians as being dismantlers of communism and the standard bearers of democratic transition. This was down to President Bush's visit to Budapest in July 1989, which can even be called historic as it was the first time an incumbent US President had visited the Hungarian capital. Incidentally, this also indicated that Hungary's importance had grown in the eyes of Washington. Whilst Budapest – as a Soviet satellite – hadn't previously been considered as a worthwhile negotiating partner, from 1989 onwards Hungary was considered as a partner and even a potential ally.

At the time of the regime change, Hungarian-American relations were reborn under a lucky star. Hungary was the positive example, one of Washington's favourites. I personally had the opportunity to experience that not only members of the administration sympathised with us, but their friendly feelings were shared by academics and members of the media elite, staff of important thinktanks, civil society organisations, foundation leaders; in short, almost everyone who matters when it comes to bilateral relations. Figuratively speaking, Hungarian leaders passed each other the baton in Washington. In May 1990, Árpád Göncz, still only as interim president, was greeted by President Bush, followed by a successful official visit by Prime Minister József Antall in October. A distinctly friendly relationship was established between Antall and President Bush, and to this day Antall is the only Hungarian leader to have a truly good personal relationship with an incumbent American president.

President Clinton visited Hungary twice: in 1994 and 1996, albeit it's true that his second brief visit wasn't primarily for us but for the American air base in Taszár. For a long time, official visits of Hungarian leaders to Washington were both commonplace and regular. President Árpád Göncz in 1999, Prime Minister Viktor Orbán in 1998, Prime Minister Péter Medgyessy twice (in 2002 and 2004), Ferenc Gyurcsány in 2005, and Gordon Bajnai in 2009, all paid visits to the American capital, albeit Bajnai was 'only' received by then Vice President Joe Biden, but this visit was, on the American side, considered to have been especially successful. Meanwhile, U.S. President George W. Bush also visited Hungary in 2006; so far, the last presidential visit to the country.

The political elite of the regime change, especially its members involved in foreign policy, had a clear Atlanticist commitment and this preference was strongly reflected in our foreign policy. Thanks to this, Hungary was able to join NATO in the first round, in 1999, alongside Poland and the Czech Republic. Hungary elected for an Atlantic orientation even amidst delicate and difficult situations. In 1999, Hungary supported NATO's Kosovo operation, Hungarian airspace and the Taszár air base being used by the allies in military operations against Serbia despite the fact that the hundreds of thousands of Hungarians in the Vojvodina were effectively Milošević's hostages, and that he used this to attempt to blackmail the Hungarian leadership. We participated, to the best of our ability, in every mission that was important for the United States, including SFOR in Bosnia, KFOR in Kosovo, the NATO mission in Afghanistan, and the peacekeeping mission in Iraq.

Hungary was the ally who could be counted on even in difficult times, and who itself could count on the support of the United States should it require it.

The decade and a half following the change of regime was the heyday of Hungarian-American relations. Unfortunately, this special and valuable period came to an end after 2006, and then slowly began to erode.

There were worrying signs in the foreign policy orientation of the Gyurcsány government after 2006. The hitherto committedly Atlanticist policy appeared to be slowly replaced by a shifting, wishy-washy political manouevering which seeks strategic relations with the Russians and is basically characteristic of our current foreign policy. Gyurcsány spectacularly neglected the Nabucco gas pipeline plan called for by the Americans and supported the rival South Stream project linked to Gazprom. He sold Malév, the national airline, to a dubious Russian businessman under suspicious circumstances, initiated preliminary negotiations on the construction of the Paks 2 nuclear power plant, even avoided a clear stance in favour of the pro-Western forces in the Ukrainian conflict, offered only half-hearted condemnation of Putin's aggression towards Georgia and, during a short period held numerous mysterious meetings with President Putin, the subject and outcomes of which remain unknown to the outside world. All this had consequences for Hungarian-American relations. Initially, it was considered only a momentary derailment, but later, the reset in Hungarian foreign policy orientation was increasingly considered to constitute a substantial shift.

In this situation, the opposition at the time and its leading party, Fidesz, were greatly appreciated by the US administration. Viktor Orbán recognised the moment with his excellent sense of timing, and during this period became the main defender of Western values and orientation, and a keen critic of Hungary's uncertain foreign policy. In a series of memorable speeches he eloquently castigated the government's mistaken policy, defended the Nabucco pipeline plan, and attacked South Stream and the planned expansion of the Paks nuclear power plant, dubbing his rival Putin's lap dog.

It's no exaggeration to say that Viktor Orbán was one of the favourites of the then American ambassador April Foley; she was a real fan, all the while her and the incumbent Prime Minister couldn't abide each other. Not only Foley, but also her successor as American Ambassador, Eleni Kounalakis, had a particularly positive opinion of Viktor Orbán in the beginning. I myself witnessed her when she likened Orbán directly to Bill Clinton in a private conversation, and for her there was greater recognition than that. She saw in him a successful and talented self-made man who didn't belong to the traditional elite, and this type of politician is especially valued by Americans.

The 2010 election brought a radical domestic political turn and provided the basis for the second Orbán government to start with a clean slate and regain the goodwill and support of the Western world. Unfortunately, the necessary and expected correction didn't occur. On the contrary, the foreign and domestic policies of the Orbán government have increasingly distanced and alienated our country from its allies, especially the United States. This erosion process has accelerated, and now has far-reaching consequences.

The real drama in the field of Hungarian-American relations lies deep under the surface though. Journalists, but often even analysts, usually pay attention only to the surface; the nature and frequency of visits between the two countries, what is said in the official statements, and so forth. These, of course, also hold their own significance in diplomacy but, much more severe than our spectacular losses on the surface, is what has happened in the relationship's fundamentals, the sociological foundations. Unfortunately, we've largely lost the special goodwill, compassion, willingness to cooperate, the trust towards us in the infrastructure of the relationship system, in that highly important second and third line; among diplomats, experts, journalists, think tanks, and academic intellectuals working in the region who fundamentally define the United States' relationship with another country. This process of estrangement is reflected in the increasing rarity of my American invitations and appearances.

I've also sensed a clear change in the manner in which they're received. Whilst in the past the opinion of Hungarian politicians, experts and diplomats was much sought after and considered relevant not only when it came to Hungarian matters but those of the region as a whole, nowadays they aren't particularly curious as to it. In general, it can be said that interest in our country has waned, and that we've lost our previous highly favourable, almost privileged position in the region. We've the lost the solid foundations needed for good relations, and we can't make up for these through overpaid and poorly appointed lobbyists. The changes deep down are unfortunately tectonic in nature and have resulted in a fundamental rearrangement in the structure of our relationships.

It'll be exceedingly difficult for a new Hungarian leadership to regain, if indeed it can, this trust and goodwill, as it's a treasure for which many countries are competing with us. Our former privileged position was largely due to the miracle of regime change, but this treasure has been squandered over the past decade and can only be restored, if at all, through concerted effort. It's now clear that much better use should have been made of this existing political capital (trust).

The Hungarian government often argues that although relations at the political level aren't ideal, economic and military relations are excellent. It's also worth nuancing this a bit. The United States is indeed still an important trading partner and plays prominent role in Hungarian investments. At the time of the regime change they were the first to make significant investments, and we're still the beneficiaries of this golden age. It was then that GE entered the Hungarian market by acquiring Tungsram, and it's still one of the most important players in the US market albeit it has already sold a significant part of the company, and the Tungsram brand itself. It was at this time that GM Opel arrived in Szentgotthárd (which is now under French ownership), Alcoa, Ford, IBM, and Westel (which is also no longer American-owned). For a long time, the number one investor in Hungary was the United States, and it still – largely due to those early investments – holds second or third place today. There has been little significant recent investment in the past decade, whilst many have withdrawn from the Hungarian market. The only truly significant new American player that has emerged in the Hungarian market in recent years is the investment management firm BlackRock, which established a centre in Hungary in 2017. Data from recent years shows that the United States only just makes the top ten in terms of fresh new investment.

Besides the deterioration in the investor climate, the deteriorating relationship and cooling between the two countries clearly plays a role in this decline. Past good relationships also emboldened and encouraged investors, and the critical state of the relationship today has a negative impact on investment sentiment.

The deterioration in bilateral relations can basically be traced back to three reasons. The first reason is certainly Hungary's change in foreign policy orientation, its weakening Atlanticist commitment, and its foreign policy strategy called the Eastern Opening which also includes close and opaque Hungarian-Russian and Hungarian-Chinese relations. Hungary is no longer a reliable friend, but an unpredictable, reluctant ally. The second reason primarily affects economic actors: legal uncertainty, an unpredictable business environment, hostility to foreign capital, protectionism that restricts competition, and widespread corruption, often enshrined in law. Finally, the third reason is worldview: the dismantling of liberal democracy, restrictions on freedom of the press, and the building of an illiberal state and its open proclamation have also contributed to the deterioration in relations. Undoubtedly, this third reason is taken more seriously by the Democrat administration than by the Republicans, but in the second and third lines that define our relations, these are still important considerations. The – far from favourable – climate of opinion that surrounds our relations, though, is determined by this medium.

On the surface the Orbán government has already been able to make a noticeable improvement in bilateral relations, such as, for example, the procuring of Viktor Orbán's visit to Washington in May 2019. This, however, didn't bring a meaningful breakthrough in bilateral relations. One of the reasons for this is that the perception of the Hungarian government hasn't improved in the medium which determines bilateral relations. Moreover, discontinuation of the policy of Eastern Opening, as called for by the Americans with special regard to its ideological and foreign policy aspects, the reassessment of the close and opaque Hungarian-Russian relations, the proclamation of a clear Western orientation, the cessation of discriminatory action against American interests (such as the CEU), and restricting Chinese technology and communications companies (especially Huawei and ZTE), hasn't taken place.

Thus, for tactical reasons the relationship between the two countries may even improve in the short term, but a substantial improvement in the fundamentals can only occur if Hungary addresses and remedies the real causes. Whilst these reasons persist, we can't expect a substantial improvement in our relations. We don't have to act because the Americans are demanding it or are holding us to account, but because we ourselves want to live in a country that's free from the burdens of the faulty domestic and foreign policies of recent years. We would be the primary beneficiaries of such a move, but there would also be a positive effect on our foreign relations, Hungarian-American relations included. Hungary has a much greater interest in having close cooperation and smooth relations with the United States, than vice versa.

A constructive, good relationship would increase our security, strengthen our economy, and improve our ability to assert our interests internationally. When we redesign Hungary's foreign policy strategy the renewal of this important system of relations will play a key role. We must strive to regain the favourable position we once held in the decade and a half following the change of regime. It isn't a matter of flattery, servility, or empty-gesture politicking, but a new Hungarian foreign policy that's aware of its own orientation and identity, builds its strategy upon this, and follows it consistently and predictably. The most effective way to improve our relations is to make Hungary better in all areas, both in foreign and domestic policy, and this is in our interest irrespective of Hungarian-American relations.

Russia: the re-emergence of the forgotten friend

By the end of the Cold War, the Soviet Union had already lost its superpower status, and it soon disintegrated. Russia, its number one successor, emerged only as a regional superpower. For a long time, struggling with severe internal crises, it appeared to be reconciled to this role, but since President Putin came to power the Russian leadership has been making increasingly obvious efforts to restore its former superpower status. Unfortunately, these efforts haven't been entirely in vain.

Russia's foreign policy is based on the paranoid perception that the outside world is hostile, wants to harm Russia, and threatens the country's territorial integrity and sovereignty. Russia's security is only guaranteed if it is militarily strong and other countries fear it. This isn't a new phenomenon, the fear of encirclement having already existed in the tsarist empire, and its descendants having inherited this paranoid tendency. The Soviet Union made this constant suspicion of the outside world the basic principle of the system.

Today's Russian foreign policy faithfully follows this centuries-old tradition based on imperial nationalism, representing it aggressively through a policy of force. Bismarck's description of contemporary Italy as having 'a large appetite and rotten teeth' is also very apt when it comes to Russia.

Russia considers the former Soviet republics, with the possible – although even this is nowadays no longer clear – exception of the Baltic states, to be within their own sphere of interest. It doesn't even call them sovereign independent nations but the 'near abroad', and where they are concerned it seeks a completely free hand. Until now, the outside world has only weakly and reluctantly acted against this attitude. If Russia feels its interests in this region as being threatened, it won't shy away from military intervention (see Georgia in 2008, and Ukraine in 2014).

In recent years, Russia has clearly been pursuing a revisionist policy and is one of the prime challengers to the existing liberal world order. There have been several attempts to involve Russia as a partner in maintaining world order, but these have failed due to the unpredictable, irregular behaviour of the Russian leadership. It transcends – without any inhibitions whatsoever – the rules of the international order should they constitute an obstacle to their aspirations and considers the rules to be binding only as long as it finds them favourable.

Russia continues to view NATO as a military alliance that threatens its security and sees a threat to itself in the close cooperation between the United States and its European allies, so it thus constantly works hard to dismantle this unit. Of the European countries, it attaches great importance to Germany and seeks to separate it from its allies, or at least significantly loosen Germany's commitment to Atlanticism.

In order to dismantle the internal unity and cohesion of the Western world, it needs willing, understanding partners within the EU and NATO, and for this role has primarily selected Greece and Cyprus and, secondarily, Hungary and Slovakia. Unfortunately, these attempts haven't been entirely unsuccessful among the selected countries.

Because of Russia's selfish and destructive foreign policy it has no true allies of equal standing. It is experimenting primarily with the other revisionist superpower China, and Turkey, which is turning away from the West, but these experiments have so far had mixed results. Due to a lack of mutual trust and conflicting interests we can't talk of a stable, long-term and reliable alliance. Cooperation is based on short-term interests and momentary common interests, but there is a palpable strong ambivalence on the part of the parties. Within the space of a year, for example, Russia's relations with Turkey were defined by three completely different landscapes. In 2015, the countries recognised each other as strategic partners and set out large-scale joint plans, primarily in the field of energy. There was talk of building a Russian nuclear power plant, a pipeline called Turkish Stream, and other major joint investments. By the end of the year, though, following the shooting down of a Russian military aircraft, a state of war had almost erupted between the two countries and bilateral relations had completely frozen. Then, after an unsuccessful Turkish coup attempt, relations unexpectedly warmed up again in 2016, and albeit their intensity didn't reach the pre-conflict period, the Turkish Stream project, for example, was revived. Similar, if not so strong, fluctuations can be found in Russian-Chinese relations. Trust between the parties isn't complete here either.

The majority of the former Soviet republics surround Russia as satellite states (I'm not, of course, thinking of the Baltic states, and not of Ukraine or Georgia), but the relationships are lopsided. These former Soviet republics are dependent on Russia in all respects. Their economies are closely intertwined with that of Russia, their goods reach other markets often only through Russia, and Russian mediation, and many are also politically dependent on the support of the Russian leadership. This is especially true for the post-communist states of Central Asia, whose external and internal security, and stability, are all guaranteed by Russia.

Russia's relationship with the West has traditionally been ambivalent. The West is partly admired and seen as an example to be followed, and partly as a suspicious and dangerous enemy. Russia's foreign policy also reflected this duality for a long time.

It couldn't decide whether it wanted constructive cooperation, or whether would appear as a rival; a challenger. This duality of policy manifests itself not only alternately, but often in parallel.

At the same time, since 2014 at the latest, the dominant role determining Russian foreign policy has been that of challenger. Part of this is the officially proclaimed doctrine of 'hybrid warfare' against the West. Within this, a non-declared hybrid war began which seeks to, through a wide variety of means, weaken Western countries that are considered rivals. Russia has carved out a significant lead in the field of cyber warfare and also hasn't been slow in taking advantage of it. All sorts of plots are afoot, from the hacking of computer systems to espionage, as well is the compromising and playing off of political actors. An important part of the hybrid warfare is the propaganda war. Recognising the weaknesses and ineffectiveness of former communist propaganda, the primary goal today isn't to spread positive news about Russia, but rather to create confusion, spread fake news, moral panic, and undermine society's sense of security. Numerous fake news sites, a substantial army of paid trolls and journalists, Facebook groups, and blogs, serve this purpose. In the spirit of hybrid warfare, they support various extremist movements, populist parties, eurosceptic views, secessionist aspirations and anti-refugee sentiments, and even took an active role in influencing the Brexit campaign and the 2016 US presidential election, to the extent that even influenced the end results. Russian strategists operate on the basis of a comprehensive plan and do anything that's detrimental to the Western socio-political system and that weakens the West. With the West not being in the slightest bit prepared for this attack, and also only recognising it belatedly, Russia has achieved significant success in this area. Western leaders have only awakened to the danger and become aware of this new challenge in the past couple of years.

Russia committed itself to a bold step in the autumn of 2015. Military intervention in Syria marks a new level of politicisation of Russian power. For the first time since 1991, Russian forces were deployed beyond the borders of the former Soviet Union. With its intervention in Syria it has built itself a strong position in the Middle East, where Russia hadn't really been seen as a player in the past two decades. This has now fundamentally changed, and today Russia has become an unavoidable factor in the Syrian conflict. Russian intervention reversed the military situation in Syria, propping up the dictatorial power of President Assad – who'd previously been all but defeated – and making him the de facto winner of the civil war. Although far from happy, Westerners have been forced to accept this, and expect Russia to participate in the settlement process.

Neither was confidence in Russia's intentions boosted by President Putin's announcement on 1 March 2018, of new Russian 'miracle weapons'. In his annual state of the nation address he even illustrated, using video footage, the new superweapons – a 2,000-kilometer-range hypersonic cruise missile launchable from an airplane, a nuclear-powered 'unlimited range' hypersonic ballistic missile, and a supersonic nuclear-powered drone submarine – which he described as being invincible. Although Putin claimed that these weapons are needed to maintain world peace, it's striking that all are explicitly offensive weapons. He added that Russia would view a possible attack on any of its allies as an attack on itself and would respond accordingly. All these steps support the clear revisionist ambitions and aspirations of the Russian leadership to regain superpower status.

The Western nations aren't united in appraising Russia's aspirations for power and influence. The desire for appeasement and reconciliation can be felt on the part of some countries, one sign of which is that more and more people want to abolish or substantially reduce the sanctions imposed for the occupation of the Crimea. Hungary holds the dubious honour of being one of the first, and leading countries calling for the reduction of sanctions, albeit it never prevented their extension.

The Russian economy has been plunged into recession for many years, the main reason of which wasn't the international sanctions but the low price of oil and natural gas. Russia's export revenues decreased by 35% in 2015. They succeeded in avoiding collapse because they held significant financial reserves from previous years when energy prices were high. Many expected that the Russian economy would plunge into serious crisis after a few years' time as a result of persistently low oil and natural gas prices. This didn't happen, however. In part, energy prices began to rise, in part, other commodity prices were more favourable and, in part, the resilience of the Russian economy and the tolerance of Russian society to deteriorating conditions were significantly greater than expected. Thus, the expectation that Russia could be forced to its knees economically wasn't realised.

At the same time, protracted economic difficulties and internal decline accelerated by the coronavirus epidemic, have challenged President Putin's popularity and the internal stability of his regime. By 2020, the decline of the system has become increasingly clear. Although a dubious referendum and decision by the Constitutional Court in principle allows Putin to remain in office until 2036, I wouldn't bet my house on this happening.

Sensing the increasingly serious problems, the Russian leadership signalled its intention to settle deteriorating East-West relations on via several channels. This could pave the way for a consolidation in Russian-Western relations, for a fresh start which could also have a positive geostrategic effect. Distancing Russia from China and achieving success on the issue of East-West cooperation would be a particularly positive development that would stabilise the security situation. No substantive steps, though, have been taken in this respect as of late 2020.

Hungarian-Russian relations

Russia has traditionally been an important economic partner for Hungary. It has a particularly important role in Hungary's oil and gas supply and is a potentially promising market for Hungarian agriculture, albeit it's true that for a long time this has been an unfulfilled promise (we failed to make use of the opportunity even before the sanctions).

Our energy dependence tends to be overestimated by many, especially by the government. We can, in fact, increasingly now talk about interdependence, because it's also in Russia's basic interest to be able to sell its reserves as this is its most important export. We've now greatly reduced our previously one-sided energy dependence. We could satisfy all our crude oil needs from the free market via the Adriatic pipeline, whereas for natural gas we can supply more than two thirds of our needs independently of Russia via the Baumgarten pipeline and through the Hungarian-Slovakia interconnector, as well as via domestic extraction.

Unfortunately, according to government plans our energy dependence isn't planned to decrease further in the near future, but rather to increase to the tune of another important element. It's undeniable that the construction of the Paks 2 nuclear power plant is a big business opportunity for Rosatom. It's highly debatable, though, that we really need this power plant. There are serious arguments against new nuclear investment. These are partly environmental, partly power plant safety, and partly economic arguments but, due to the secrecy of the contract, the risks of corruption can't be ruled out either. The strongest counter-argument, though, is national security. Due to the operation, servicing and fuel supply of the power plant we'll be dependent on Russia for decades to come. I'm convinced that Hungary doesn't need Paks 2 in this form. Now, when there's a real revolution going on in renewable energy in any case, it would constitute a real mistake to commit to the nuclear option, not to mention Hungary's long-term vulnerability and dependence on Russia.

Russia is *the* key partner in the policy of Eastern Opening announced by the third Orbán government. In his 2014 speech in Băile Tușnad, Orbán called Russia a star of international analysis from which we and Western Europe have much to learn. Viktor Orbán is probably impressed by President Putin and the system he has established. This is only partly explained by the fact that their personalities share many common traits. At the same time, the government's policy towards Russia is part of the separate path policy of opportunism; the so-called peacock dance. The Hungarian government also intends to play a tactical role in Russia's foreign policy, signalling that if we don't need the West, we have other options. That is, it's part of the government's bargaining potential or, to put it more bluntly, also its blackmail potential.

Today, it's no longer a particularly brave assertion to say that the government's rainbow-chasing policy of Eastern Opening, Hungarian-Russian relations included, has failed. The government fantasised about a significant increase in trade, as opposed to the approximate 30% decline which ensued in the bilateral relationship. This is only partly explained by the sanctions, and the measures Russia introduced in response.

From the moment they were introduced, the Hungarian government has been sharply critical of sanctions against Russia. Viktor Orbán stated in the summer of 2014 that we've shot ourselves in the foot and has been constantly advocating the abolition of the sanctions ever since. It's true, though, that when the Council of Europe decided to extend the sanctions on a rolling six-month basis, he never opposed the extension. He once said that his reason for not doing so was that it would have disrupted EU unity. Contrary to public opinion and propaganda, the sanctions didn't have a significant effect on Hungarian exports. Our agricultural exports were only partially affected and, fortunately, Hungarian exporters adapted very well to the changed situation, finding new markets in place of Russia. For such reasons, we haven't been able to prove that we've suffered heavy losses as a result of the sanctions, so we thus haven't even received EU compensation. Poland and Lithuania, on the other hand, have suffered verifiable and spectacular losses and they've been entitled to claim partial compensation from the EU. This is why it's incomprehensible to our partners why it's so important for the Hungarian government to have the sanctions lifted.

Distrust in the Hungarian government's intentions has also been fuelled by the fact that Hungary reacted extremely leniently and tolerantly to the annexation of Crimea, and developments in eastern Ukraine where separatists backed by the Russian state grossly violated the territorial integrity of our neighbour. The official reaction to the Ukrainian Law on Education, with Hungary consistently obstructing and impeding Ukraine's Euro-Atlantic integration efforts until the law is repealed, is also considered excessive. It isn't disputed that the provision of the Ukrainian Law on Education on the use of the mother-tongue severely restricts the fundamental right of nationalities to education in their mother-tongue. Nevertheless, there was incomprehension as to why the Hungarian government didn't address this issue on a bilateral basis or seek to jointly settle it along with its fellow NATO allies – Poland and Romania – who're also directly affected, as well as to why it acted so vehemently on a matter which external observers consider, in its current form, to primarily be a Russian issue not a Hungarian one. It's undoubtedly difficult to work out what the actual drivers of these governmental actions are, as well as identify the real Hungarian interests behind them.

It can be concluded that Hungary has so far gained very little tangible benefit from its political flirting with Russia. For a long time we received natural gas more expensively than Poland, which is far from friendly with the Russians, and neither have we been exempt from the Russian counter-sanctions, and so forth. The currying of Russian favour hasn't served any Hungarian interest. On the other hand, it has caused very perceptible damage to Hungary's international reputation and relations with its allies. This Russia policy also played a noticeable role in the cooling of Hungarian-American relations, but it also burdens Hungarian-Polish and Hungarian-Baltic relations. It's no coincidence that our country is mentioned by renowned analysts and important organs of the world press as the Russians' Trojan Horse or the weakest link in the Western alliance system. For this reason, Ludovic Orban, later Romania's prime minister, once candidly dubbed Hungary 'NATO's festering ulcer'.

No one of course wants the Hungarian government to take the lead in a Cold War crusade, and for Hungarian leaders to act in Cato the Elder style and constantly draw attention to the danger that Russia poses. That would be a thankless task in any case, and there are much more credible volunteers for the role than us. It's my opinion that there's a need for a pragmatic, transparent, mutually beneficial, equal relationship between the two countries that is free from ideology and serves the interests of the Hungarian economy. At a political level, no form of special or privileged relationship has justification. It's in Hungary's basic interest to avoid even the appearance of filling the thankless role of Trojan Horse.

We've no interest in upsetting the cohesion between Western countries, or in loosening ties with our allies. On the contrary, it's in our interest that these ties be stronger than ever in these difficult times of crisis. We must therefore take the utmost care not to appear to be representatives of Russian interests in Europe, but rather, to be the representatives of Hungarian and European interests, even against Moscow.

China and Hungary

Today, China can no longer be left out of any serious foreign policy or geostrategic analysis. It's no longer just an economic behemoth, but also a giant in world politics. It for a long time concealed its real global political ambitions, but today openly advertises and is proud of them.

China is also a revisionist power but treads a different path to Russia. It has the time and patience to wait until its time comes. China is also dissatisfied with the current world order and balance of power. It makes no secret of this but strives to follow the written and unwritten rules of international law and seeks to strengthen its position within the confines of the rules.

China's influence and prestige, unlike Russia's, is mainly due to its economic performance, although its military capabilities – which can be attributed to the intensive military development programme launched in recent years – are also remarkable. The Chinese economy has developed at a dizzying pace in recent decades, producing double-digit annual growth over a long period of time. This unbounded economic growth has slowed since the financial crisis but, until recently, the economy was still characterized by an enviable growth rate of 6-8%.

Because of the coronavirus epidemic, in the first half of 2020 – for the first time in thirty years – the performance of China's economy declined significantly (a 6.5-7% decline) but, as yet, we don't know whether this is a temporary recession or will be a longer-term trend. Even so, China now boasts the world's second strongest economy, and in the past twenty years has, almost every year, overtaken a developed economy, most recently Germany and then Japan, and it already has the United States in its sights. In terms of purchasing power parity, its national income has already reached that of the United States, but in nominal terms this will only take place sometime after 2030, provided China can maintain a robust growth rate. These impressive figures are strongly overshadowed by the fact that the wealth generated must be shared by 1.2 billion Chinese, thus, the gross national product per capita is still, and will for a long time be, relatively low. It's been largely down to China, though (and India, of course), that the number of people living in extreme poverty in the world has fallen dramatically over the past two decades. Today, roughly one billion people getting by on less than $ 2 a day. Twenty years ago, there were twice as many.

The problem with China's national income isn't just that it's shared between so many, but also that it's distributed extremely unevenly both geographically and socially. Many fear that this could, in the foreseeable future, lead to serious social tension, possibly even unrest. For the time being the Chinese leadership is handling the situation well, but there are constant reports of minor disturbances and skirmishes born of growing inequalities and a wide range of dissatisfaction.

China's economic growth is still mainly driven by exports, but domestic consumption has recently also been playing an increasing role. It is a true export world power, having become the world's number one exporter by surpassing Germany some years ago. The export-driven economy also explains much about China's foreign policy. The country's foreign policy profile was, for a long time, markedly restrained, moderate, and conflict-avoiding. Given that exports were the primary source of its prosperity, it had a fundamental interest in avoiding, and in smoothing over conflicts and eliminating any disruption that might adversely affect its trading activities. It's also because of this that the image of China being a peaceful, compromise-ready power which doesn't pose a threat where the outside world is concerned.

The further a country is from China geographically, the more it tends to believe in this idyllic picture – the attitude of European Union leaders towards China has also been determined by this misconception until recently.

China's immediate neighbours never believed in the myth of a peaceful, gentle giant. From Mongolia to India, Vietnam, South Korea through Taiwan to Japan, there is a sense of suspicion and concern about China's supposed hidden intentions and ambitions. The oppressed minorities of the country, such as the Tibetans and the Uyghurs, have also experienced for themselves the falsehood of a peace-loving, compromise-ready, conflict-avoiding image. The Chinese leadership has already used a wide range of tools – ranging from pressure to aggressive action – against its neighbours, and Japan, Taiwan, or more recently India, have had direct experience of this.

The image of a peaceful and gentle China appeared to be supported by the fact that, for a long time, military development wasn't a priority for the Chinese leadership. This, though, is now a thing of the past. It would be a great mistake to underestimate the rapidly evolving capabilities of the Chinese People's Liberation Army in recent years. In terms of numbers, the Chinese military – with an army of nearly two and a half million permanently armed soldiers – is the largest in the world, albeit this number shouldn't be overestimated given that two thirds of them are carrying out their compulsory military service and it thus isn't a fully professional force. China's defence expenditure is 2% of GDP, which comes to about $ 150 billion a year (the exact number isn't known because part of the spending isn't included in the defence budget). According to some, actual spending could reach as much as $ 200 billion dollars (still only a third of U.S. defence spending), which would constitute by far the second largest defence budget in the world; roughly twice that of Russia and three times that of India. It's not so much the size of the amount that's worth noting, but the trend within military development. The significant yearly increase in expenditures, the rapid modernisation of the armed forces, the acquisition of new weapons systems, mainly from Russian sources but also developed by itself, is significant. Of particular note is the priority development of the Air Force and Navy, which may in the near future facilitate the use of military force and the deployment of an expeditionary force far from China's borders. To this end, China has verifiably developed new stealth aircraft and other hypersonic aircraft and missiles, the Chinese Navy ordered two aircraft carriers, it began building artificial islands and military bases in the South China Sea, and set up a naval base in Djibouti in the Gulf of Aden – the entrance to the Red Sea, one of the most important commercial routes –, thousands of kilometres from its borders. These developments haven't escaped the attention of geostrategic analysts, who have for years viewed the frightening development of China's military capabilities as a new security risk.

The construction of artificial islands in the South China Sea and the establishment of military bases there have also elicited serious concern from the leaders of the countries affected, and the United States. This aggressive military expansion, which is otherwise illegitimate under international law, raises the prospect that China might even also be able to take full control of one of the most important maritime routes in world trade. In addition, the bases now established could pose a direct threat to the security of the surrounding countries of Burma, Vietnam, and the Philippines.

China's robust economic and global political efforts are served by a gigantic development strategy called the Belt and Road Initiative (BRI), which replaced the original New Silk Road infrastructure programme. The primary goal of the initiative, financed mainly by Chinese government loans, is the infrastructural development of the Eurasian region; that is, the acceleration and facilitation of market access for Chinese goods. The programme focuses primarily on the development of transport infrastructure, i.e., the construction and modernisation of railways, roads, ports and airports, mainly in Asia and, in a small part, Africa. The programme has several objectives, and the funding for the infrastructural development will be provided by Chinese loans, which will allow the business-based placement of significant Chinese cash reserves. The investments are also conditional on the significant participation of Chinese contractors and suppliers in their implementation. With the Chinese construction industry now experiencing significant spare capacity stemming from the years of exceptionally high growth, this can be utilised via the export of services, thus also solving the issue of overcapacity. This scheme is particularly favourable for countries which can only access credit with great difficulty or at exceedingly high interest rates on international financial markets, or which don't have the capacity to implement it. Thus, it's primarily developing countries that stand in line for these developments. There are also concealed political conditions where participation is concerned. This became clear in the case of Pakistan when the Chinese unexpectedly halted the planned investment for political reasons.

India and the United States have watched this gigantic project with suspicious from the start, because within it they saw China's covert expansionary aspirations. Indian leaders candidly called the programme Chinese colonisation. This is certainly an exaggeration, but it's indisputable that China also wants to increase its political influence in the countries concerned through loans and investments.

The Belt and Road Initiative already lost momentum in 2019 and, in 2020, in no small part due to the coronavirus epidemic, it ground to a halt. The reasons are manifold. On the one hand, several of the beneficiary countries, citing economic difficulties, have requested a rescheduling and deferral of loans (Pakistan, Sri Lanka, Nigeria, and Ghana), and on the other, the Chinese economy is in recession and resources are needed to kickstart the Chinese economy. Critical voices have also emerged within China about the project. More and more people are questioning its benefits and practicability. There is a sense of intent on the part of the Chinese leadership to redesign the project, with more and more new, less expensive Digital BRI and, more recently, Health BRI programmes are being insisted upon, at the expense of previously favoured, costly infrastructure investments.

Chinese President Xi Jinping surprised his audience at the 2017 World Economic Forum in Davos by offering a vigorous defence of free trade. The unofficial title of defender of global free trade had, indisputably, previously been the incumbent president of the United States, but Trump, though, openly went against the American free trade tradition and proclaimed a protectionist, nationalist, egotistical trade policy. Xi Jinping immediately announced his wish to take over the unoccupied mantle of standard bearer for free trade. China's commitment to the principles of free trade, though, cannot be considered sincere. There's no doubt that, as an export power, it has an interest in liberalising world trade as much as possible, but China's internal market is still very much a closed one with many bureaucratic and legal barriers, official measures that hamper free trade and foreign investment, and intellectual property lacks satisfactory protection. All the while the Chinese leadership calls for further liberalisation in world trade, it shows no sign of liberalising and opening its internal market to foreign traders and investors.

The 19th National Congress of the Chinese Communist Party, held in October 2017 amidst much fanfare, was an especially important event in Chinese domestic politics. There were signs beforehand that this would be no ordinary party congress, and it certainly wasn't. Five of the seven members of the standing Politburo Committee were replaced, strictly by new members loyal to Xi Jinping. The Chinese premier gave three-and-a-half-hour rousing, fiery speech, broadcast live nationwide, outlining his Xi Jinping Thought on Socialism with Chinese characteristics for a New Era ('Xi Jinping Thought' for short). The development of military capabilities was given a prominent place in his vision. "We're developing the army to fight," he said, adding that "Our army must be able to win when the time comes." In his speech, he touched upon the importance of naval facilities in the South China Sea and also praised the Belt and Road Initiative. The most important parts of his vision were also enshrined in the party constitution, **the first time since Mao Zedong and Deng Xiaoping that a Chinese leader has had an ideology named after him in the constitution.** The dictatorial ambitions of the Chinese leader are reinforced by the March 2018 amendment to the constitution and which abolished the restricting of the presidency to two terms, meaning that President Xi Jinping could remain the country's number one leader indefinitely. It's a sure message that, after a few decades of transition, China will once again have a leader with Mao-like total power.

This doesn't augur well for the outside world. It should be remembered that under Secretary-General Mao, China's conflicts – of which there were many – were often solved militarily. Tibet was invaded in 1950, and one million Chinese 'volunteers' took part in the Korean War, on the Northern side, between 1950 and 1953. The Tibetan uprising was brutally quashed in 1959, war was waged against India in 1962, followed again by an armed border conflict in 1967 over the Indian protectorate of Sikkim, and then the Sino-Soviet border conflict – launched without a declaration of war – in 1969 along the Ussuri River.

It of course doesn't follow that Xi Jinping necessarily intends to resolve his conflicts by military force, but we can't be certain that he'll necessarily avoid such a solution to prospective conflicts. Assertive Chinese foreign policy in early 2020 shows that the Chinese leadership isn't deterred by aggressive action either. China openly threatened Taiwan, firmly clamped down on Hong Kong's hitherto respected quasi-democratic system, embarked on a border conflict with India, acted aggressively against Australia, and escalated the war of words with Japan. The previous conflict-avoiding, compromise-seeking foreign policy would appear to have been pushed into the background.

Self-deception based upon a false sense of security, and irresponsible panic, are both misguided. China isn't an enemy to the Western world, but a key partner. It's in our interest to keep it that way, but it doesn't just depend on us. The Chinese leadership must understand that a good relationship is based on mutual goodwill and trust. If the trust is shaken, then the good relationship is also over. There are numerous signs that we need to acquire proof of the Chinese leadership's goodwill.

It's in the world's interest that it encourages China to become involved in maintaining an international order based on the rule of law. It's also in China's interest. China needs to clarify whether it wants to be one of the pillars of the current order (as if it were in its interest to support free trade) or whether it wants to create a new order based on the Chinese model. If it chooses the former, it will acquire a greater say, an increased ability to assert its interests, but will also have to be more accommodating. The benefits from this far outweigh what China can expect from the latter option; the undoing of the current world order and the enforcement of a new one. Not to mention that such a process could easily slip out of the control of all concerned and destroy all order in the world.

Hungarian-Chinese relations

Following the change of regime, the 1989 Tiananmen Square massacre and subsequent clamp down cast a long shadow over Hungarian-Chinese relations. In the countries of transition, Hungary included, the brutal reaction of the Chinese leadership to democratisation efforts provoked understandable resentment. The Hungarian opposition in 1989, which is largely the same as the post-1990 political elite, understandably identified with the protesting students, and found the regime's harsh retribution against the protesters unacceptable.

Considering this, it's no wonder that the first high-level meeting between the leaders of the two countries took place only in 1994, during the official visit of President Árpád Göncz to Beijing. This was soon followed by President Jiang Zemin's official visit to Budapest in 1995. This visit was surrounded by exaggerated expectations on the part of the Hungarian side, but these proved to be a false hope. Although many promising announcements have been made, large-scale plans presented, and letters of intent signed, there has been no real breakthrough in bilateral relations.

The first Orbán government was distant from China. Ideological standpoints played an important role in this, as did the unfavourable experience of previous years' dashed hopes. No high-level meetings took place during this period, and Antal Rogán, on behalf of the Anti-Dictatorship Action Group, even asked the government and the parliament not to pay official visits to countries deemed to be dictatorships, and not to receive delegations from them. Fidesz even fulfilled this demand in their first term of government. The extent of the later turnaround is indicated by the fact that after 2010, the very same Antal Rogán became chairman of the Hungarian-Chinese friendship section of parliament.

Viktor Orbán – unofficially – even received the Dalai Lama, and the government agreed to the visit of Taiwanese Vice President Anett Lu to Budapest, which led to a sharp diplomatic standoff between Budapest and Beijing in the spring of 2002.

Péter Medgyessy – in 2003 – was the first Hungarian Prime Minister to visit Beijing following the regime change, and he at the same time announced strategic relations with China. We can consider this meeting as a turning point in the history of bilateral relations, as from here on, regardless of who the government was, high-level visits have been regular and economic relations have developed almost unbroken, apart from a decline in the few years following the 2008 financial crisis. President Hu Jintao visited Budapest in 2004, Prime Minister Ferenc Gyurcsány visited China in 2005 and 2007, and then current president Xi Jinping – vice president at the time – honoured us with a visit in 2009.

The bilateral relationship, though, gained real momentum in 2011, and this was related to the policy of Eastern Opening officially announced at the time. This is the Orbán government's comprehensive foreign policy and international trade strategy, which grants China a position of privilege. This change of direction was celebrated by the visit to Budapest of the then Chinese Prime Minister Wen Jiabao, which also gave the outward appearance of revealing the Hungarian government's servile commitment to its strategic partner.

In February 2014, Viktor Orbán even took half of the Hungarian government with him to Beijing, where he was also received by the Chinese president. In the spring of 2017, Viktor Orbán laid a wreath at the monument to the communist heroes in Tiananmen Square during his next visit to Beijing, and then in November of the same year, Budapest hosted Prime Minister Li Keqiang and a meeting of leaders from China and sixteen Central and Eastern European countries. At the same time, the contract for the modernisation of the Budapest-Belgrade railway line, which had been on the agenda since the visit to Beijing in 2014, was also ceremoniously signed.

Members of the government are proud to mention that Hungarian-Chinese relations have never been so good; there have never been such high-level visits between the two countries, and there has never been so much mutual praise between the leaders of the two countries. This is also true, but the question is, who really benefits, and how much does Hungary gain from this? There are serious doubts about this.

In Viktor Orbán's much quoted 2014 Băile Tușnad speech, in which he proclaimed the goal of building an illiberal state, he called China one of the stars (along with Russia and Turkey) of international analyses. China is one of the two most important partners in the strategy of Eastern Opening. The Eastern Opening is mistaken by many as a foreign trade strategy, but that's only one of the strategy's pillars, and not the most important one. Both the ideological pillar (illiberal state), and the foreign policy pillar (reorientation) play a much more important role in the strategy, and the government has been much more successful in this field than in its foreign trade aspirations. China was assigned an important role in all three pillars.

Orbán isn't the first Hungarian politician to approach Hungarian-Chinese relations with over-inflated hopes and illusions. The first signs of this could already be observed during the Horn government, but these were soon dashed as the hoped-for economic results didn't materialise. Prime Minister Péter Medgyessy, who to this day diligently works in developing bilateral relations, played a pioneering role in reviving and nurturing the illusion that the bilateral relations system is an exceptional take-off point and a repository of unlimited possibilities for the Hungarian economy. This illusion was also readily nurtured by the Chinese partners. It's no coincidence that all of Medgyessy's successors have been held captive by this illusion, and we now have to pay a heavy price for our chasing of rainbows.

Anyone who has been to China in an official capacity in the recent past has a hard time forgetting the hypnotic effects of what they see there. If you've experienced the dynamic, pulsating development, modern skyscrapers, and 21st century achievements of Beijing, Shanghai or the Shenzhen zone, you get a real sense that China is already living in the future and is far ahead of us. Never mind catching up; we can't even keep up with it. The sheer size of the country, and its dynamism, are rightly dazzling, especially to the representative of a small or medium-sized country, and it isn't without basis that you can feel that this is the future of humanity and that we mustn't miss out on it. Half of the world is jostling there and practically everyone wants to get a piece of the huge market and the big business opportunities available. The hosts perfectly understand that they need to dazzle guests and make them believe that they, too, have to somehow jump on the bandwagon.

Under the influence of dizzying experiences and impressions, few assess soberly and objectively what opportunities this market and the bilateral relationship actually hold for them. Most of our leaders don't seem to be able to face this objectively either. They have a great responsibility for the rainbow chase that characterises Hungarian-Chinese policy. For a decade and a half now, three unfounded illusions have defined the hopes of leading Hungarian politicians for China. They hope that:

– Hungary can be China's economic gateway, a bridgehead in the region,
– Hungary will be a recipient of significant Chinese investments,
– A significant market will open up in China for Hungarian-owned operators.

Unfortunately, all three assumptions are devoid of reality. It's worth taking a quick look at what the reason for this might be. The sad reality is that for China, our region as a whole isn't that important and, within this, Hungary doesn't hold any privileged position. Additionally, almost all countries in the region are applying for the role of being China's regional hub, and some have significantly better chances than us. China is also fostering competition between them, and if there will at all be such a regional hub, it'll be where investment and economic interests dictate. This won't be decided primarily by political, but by economic considerations. Presently, Poland is in a significantly better, and the Czech Republic is in a slightly better position, than us. Neither of these two countries, though, can be called the China's regional hub, and it remains questionable whether China has any need for one.

Investment figures also reflect the fact that the region isn't a priority for the Chinese economy, it accounting for only a fraction (4% according to the latest available data) of Chinese investment in Europe. If we look at the total value of investment so far, we aren't in a bad position in our region, except that most of these investments were made before 2010. The two most significant Chinese investors to date are Wanhua Holding, which acquired Borsodchem in 2010, the other being Huawei, which established its logistics centre in Biatorbágy in 2009. Many promises have been made since then, but very few significant investments have been realised. In recent years, we've been a particularly bad position in the otherwise insignificant Chinese investment in the region, with not just Poland and the Czech Republic, but also Romania and Bulgaria ahead of us in 2016, and only 6.4% of investments in the region being made in Hungary. It's worth coming to terms with the illusions, but that doesn't mean that we don't have to do everything we can to attract Chinese investment here, just that we mustn't have excessive hopes for it.

There's no doubt that China is a huge market and every country wants to get the most out of this. It's a natural and correct endeavour, but it doesn't hurt us to also be aware of the realities here. Although China still has a very significant bilateral trade surplus, Hungary doesn't appear to be performing badly in this area, and Hungarian exports are growing dynamically. This is by all accounts positive, even if we know that more than 90% of Hungarian exports aren't produced by Hungarian companies, but primarily by multinational firms. Machinery and transport equipment accounts for 80% of Hungarian exports, with almost 40% coming from vehicle engines. It's in the interest – and is the task – of Hungarian trade policy to primarily provide assistance in the market access of Hungarian-owned companies. Multinational companies don't really require the help of the Hungarian government, and neither do they ask for it; they have an independent market strategy and solve their problems by themselves. Should they encounter difficulties they don't primarily expect a solution from Hungary, but from international organisations or from the country where the parent company is registered. Thus, our trade policy should primarily aimed at increasing the market opportunities of Hungarian-owned companies. It hasn't done this with much success so far but let us be objective: this is only partly a consequence of the poor strategy. For most Hungarian-owned companies, the Chinese market isn't a priority for several reasons. On the one hand, there are few truly competitive products, the long distance is a serious obstacle for small and medium-sized enterprises, and they have volume constraints and are unable to produce the amount that the huge Chinese market demands. The correct Hungarian foreign economic policy would instead focus more on those markets where we hold comparative advantage; where Hungarian-owned companies have better opportunities and have already felt at home and operated successfully.

The truth is that the strategy of Eastern Opening has had almost no perceptible effect on the achievement of the three main objectives. We could also say that there's been a lot of fuss about nothing. All the contradictions of these efforts are borne by the latest flagship of Hungarian-Chinese relations; the project to modernise the Budapest-Belgrade railway line. This is a fine example of the harmful consequences of political voluntarism. Incidentally, this plan is part of the already-mentioned Chinese Belt and Road Initiative. We receive a Chinese loan at – according to many – an unfavourable interest rate (the loan agreement has been made an official secret for ten years so we don't know the exact details), and the Budapest-Belgrade section, on which the current capacity isn't fully utilised, will be built largely by Chinese contractors.

The estimated cost of HUF 700 billion seems to be greatly overpriced; the cost per kilometre being one of the highest in Europe at two to three times more per kilometre than in other Hungarian railway development. The recovery of the cost of the investment is completely uncertain, and according to some calculations it would take a minimum of 130 years, but possibly even up to 2,400 years. It's clear that this is primarily in the interest of the Chinese side as they can finance an investment, on favourable interest terms, that is largely implemented by Chinese contractors and, if completed, will allow Chinese goods to reach European markets more quickly. Additionally, the project isn't a real priority for China, but they're happy to support it because it fits well into their strategy.

Then why is it worth it for Hungary; why does the government support it? From an economic point of view, it certainly doesn't make sense. Political considerations lie behind the decision. On the one hand, the government sees this plan as the flagship of bilateral relations. The rationality behind it isn't economic, but political: it isn't really an investment in infrastructure, but an investment in bilateral relations, aimed at gaining the goodwill and attention of the Chinese.

On the other hand, the Eastern Opening has so far had no tangible, spectacular results – the government are already eager to present a giant investment as the undoubted success of the strategy. If there's no prospect of this on a market basis, it'll be done with taxpayers' money. In short, this is the anatomy of the Budapest-Belgrade railway modernisation plan, which is a prime example for all the flaws in the strategy of Eastern Opening. Economically, the project is pointless, but what's worse is that it doesn't make political sense either because it's a gesture that the Chinese don't particularly need, and we can't even count on their subsequent gratitude.

What does all this mean for Hungarian-Chinese relations? By no means should we consider them to be an insignificant relationship of secondary importance. We should also deal with this relationship in its rightful place. We must shed the unfounded illusions, but we mustn't underestimate or neglect the relationship either. China is an important economic partner and is playing an increasingly important role in world politics, but it won't solve all our problems. It isn't an alternative to the Western system of relations and doesn't constitute a great take-off point but an important part of the global diversification of Hungarian economic interests.

In our bilateral relations, primarily mutual economic interests must prevail – but without exaggerating or underestimating their importance. It's time to give up on servile flattery because it really doesn't bring us anything but shame and humiliation. We don't need politically motivated prestige investments, so it would be expedient to cancel the Budapest-Belgrade railway project as there is no reasonable Hungarian interest behind it.

We don't need to reinvent the wheel. Our regional counterparts Poland and the Czech Republic, who in recent years have received more investment from, and traded more with China than us, have achieved all this without grovelling and humiliation, and without the loudly announced Eastern Opening. The strategy of Eastern Opening doesn't help in this field either but, rather, hinders the establishment of a balanced system of relations based on mutual benefit. Instead of an ideological Eastern Opening, we need a pragmatic, consistent, equal partnership with China.

Part III.

Diplomacy as the most important foreign policy tool

Diplomacy, diplomats, and institutional conditions

Diplomacy is often called the second oldest profession. The history of diplomacy wouldn't fill a book but an entire library. I have neither the capacity nor sufficient knowledge or, above all, the courage to present even just an outline of the history of diplomacy. Here, I'll touch only briefly upon the role, tasks, and requirements of modern diplomacy.

The radical political, economic, social, and especially technological changes of recent decades have put good old, proven classical diplomacy out to pasture and replaced it by modern diplomacy. On the surface, modern diplomacy differs from the classic in almost everything, but deep down, the point remains the same. The basic task of diplomacy is the external representation of the country, ensuring its interests and asserting its aspirations. Carl von Clausewitz's commonplace, but very apt view was that if diplomacy fails, its logical continuation by other means is war. Diplomacy is indeed an instrument of peace; its efforts are aimed at resolving conflicts through negotiation and compromise. Modern diplomacy has a very diverse remit, of course, and the resolution of serious international conflicts is only one of its tasks, albeit to this day remaining one of its key missions.

One of the primary tasks of classical diplomacy was described in 1604 by the adventurous British diplomat Sir Henry Wotton: *"Legatus est Vir bonus, peregré missus ad mentiendum Reipublicae causa"* ("An ambassador is an honest gentleman sent to lie abroad for the good of his country"). This was true in those days and, we could say, right up until the middle of the last century; when very little reliable, independent information was available and therefore the ambassador/diplomat was the only, or one of the most important sources of information for the host country's leaders and for public opinion. We could say that an ambassador held a monopoly in terms of information about the position of their own government and about the events taking place in their country, and they could to a great extent control and manipulate this information. Due to the scarcity of alternative sources, they controlled the flow of information in both directions and, putting it mildly, manipulated both their own government just the same as they did the host country. Some legendary diplomats also took full advantage of this opportunity. In his memoirs, Maurice Paleologue, the French ambassador to St. Petersburg, makes no secret of the extent to which he influenced both the tsarist court and his own government in order to forge a strong military alliance between the two countries.

In those days, the primary task of the ambassador and diplomats was to convey and interpret the relevant information to the host country, and to obtain and send home information relevant to the country on whose behalf they were working. Today's diplomacy of course has a similar task, but its importance in diplomatic work is by no means salient anymore. As a result of modern mass media and the flow of information, the information itself is almost instantaneous, often reaching the appropriate bodies in the host country faster than it does the given country's diplomats. Moreover, there is no longer any monopoly on information, so diplomacy isn't the sole lord and handler of information with regards the country employing the diplomat, just one of many, and not necessarily considered an authentic source.

As for the acquisition and repatriation of the news, similar processes also take place there. It's difficult – and isn't required

– to compete with the speed and real-time nature of CNN and other communications agencies. This of course doesn't leave diplomats without work, as they still play an important role in evaluating and interpreting events based upon their country's perspectives and interests. Their point of view is, if not in all cases, often different from that of journalists or international analysts. It thus isn't the true task of the diplomat to obtain and send the news home quickly, but to quickly process and analyse it, and make proposals based upon the perspectives of the country on whose behalf they are working.

Through their contacts, a good diplomat also has access to non-public, often confidential, information. Of course, it's their duty to check and interpret this and bring it to the attention of the competent authorities via the appropriate channels. Discretion and strict adherence to the principle of protection of sources are important. It's in the basic interest to protect a confidential source because if the identity of the source is revealed, it can cause serious inconvenience to them and, as a result, the given source may become obsolete. Confidential information is transmitted home to the Centre – the so-called Back Office, in a secure way, in the hope that it doesn't fall into unauthorised hands. This, of course, is often wishful thinking. The largest leak of confidential foreign affairs information to date is linked to Julian Assange's Wikileaks portal, which, among many other leaked documents, released 250,000 U.S. diplomatic telegrams, documents, and internal analyses in 2009. This not only dealt a severe blow to the prestige of the United States, but also made the work of many diplomatic relations, agents, and informants impossible, and put some of their lives in imminent danger. Not to mention the damage caused by everyone subsequently becoming more wary of American diplomats, and even diplomats in general, as few would want to see their names and confidential conversations on a public portal.

Even before the Wikileaks scandal it wasn't easy to forge a relationship from which diplomats could obtain valuable inside information. There is always some special, often personal, reason for someone to share useful inside confidential information with a diplomat. Let's ignore those who do this for money or other personal gain, because they're no longer considered a contact, but rather an agent. A good diplomat has a good ability to make personal contacts. During conversations with close acquaintances and friends, details and background information can be gleamed that aren't necessarily secret but are also not public and can help a lot in understanding the background or driving forces behind certain events. Basically, it isn't about state secrets or highly confidential inside information, but information that can't be obtained from the public domain.

It isn't even common for a diplomat to have such connections. It's no coincidence that many people want to portray themselves in this manner. We, too, had an ambassador to Israel many, many years ago who appeared to have an enviable amount of inside information and delighted his superiors with his frequent encrypted telegrams. He was repeatedly even set as an example in front of his colleagues, who were embarrassed at unfortunately not being able to match his performance. The age of the internet brought him down though. His Hungarian colleagues discovered the true, public source of the 'confidential' information in his encrypted telegrams, in the online version of *The Jerusalem Post*. This story of course did a great deal of harm to the prestige of the person concerned, as well as shook belief in the reliability of encrypted telegrams.

In classical diplomacy, maintaining the continuity of interstate relations was also a prominent, almost exclusive task of diplomacy. Given that face-to-face meetings between state leaders were rare, ongoing contact took place almost exclusively through diplomats. This has also changed a lot thanks to the circumstances of modern diplomacy and the advances in technology. There is often a direct personal connection between leaders, especially foreign ministers. In urgent matters, foreign- and prime ministers often have a direct telephone conversation, bypassing diplomats, or sometimes they exchange text messages with each other, which very often, the diplomats serving in the given country only become aware of later, perhaps from the host country. There are few more humiliating situations for a diplomat than when (and I can say this from personal experience) the host country finds out that the diplomat doesn't possess any important information regarding the countries' bilateral relations. It also happened to me that I learned about the date of a foreign minister's visit from the protocol of the host country, and it was only officially communicated to me from Hungary a day later. Not only I was shocked by this, but so were our partners. Such increasingly frequent cases are also evidence that traditional diplomacy is no longer the exclusive-, but increasingly only one of many important channels of communication.

From these changing circumstances, some tend to draw the hasty conclusion that diplomacy is an outdated, redundant luxury. Diplomats are self-important and unnecessary people who're no longer needed in the modern age, and we probably won't even notice if they didn't exist. Many Hungarian political leaders also have this tacit opinion, and some of them even express it publicly. One of our prime ministers once excitedly said that the entire foreign ministry should be demolished, and the earth on which it once stood, salted. Suffice to say, this is an extreme position and fortunately not a common one. Nor is it a coincidence that the foreign policy of the prime minister in question was a clear failure. In contrast, whilst modern diplomacy is indeed different from classical diplomacy, it is no less important than in the past.

According to the legendary Israeli Foreign Minister Abba Eban, the great powers can afford to have weak diplomacy because they can counteract the lack of good diplomacy with military force and economic influence, but a small country needs to have excellent diplomacy because this is its only means of asserting its interests. The history of Hungarian diplomacy supports the truth of this statement. It would be a strong exaggeration to lay the blame for our historical tragedies on our diplomats, but it's a fact that we haven't had a great record in this area in the past. There have been outstanding Hungarian diplomats such as Gyula Andrássy, Miklós Bánffy, and Albert Apponyi, but we can't be proud of the performance of Hungarian diplomacy as a whole. Many partly attribute the weakness of our diplomacy to the humiliating terms of the Trianon Peace Treaty and the diplomatic isolation that followed, and partly to the skilful diplomacy of the successor states, especially highlighting the internationally recognised qualities of Romanian Foreign Minister Nicolae Titulescu. This is certainly an exaggerated stance, but it isn't entirely unfounded. It's an interesting contradiction: Hungarian historical consciousness recognises the importance of diplomacy in the past, whilst in the present we tend to devalue it. Yet today we would be in great need of diplomacy at least as effective and efficient as it was in the past.

What's the task of modern Hungarian diplomacy? Diplomacy is the primary, though not exclusive, means of implementing foreign policy strategy. Diplomacy can only be effective and successful if it implements a clear and realistic strategy. If not, diplomacy is an empty routine and a constant improvisation. Unfortunately, we've had plenty of examples of this in recent times. For a long time, our diplomacy has been devoid of a clear strategy, full of contingency, haste, and increasing dilettantism. This isn't primarily down to the diplomats being unfit for their task – albeit there are plenty of examples of this – but because strategic guidance is lacking. The details of the desirable strategy are discussed in the previous chapters of the book; here we will now discuss the technical conditions that are essential for the effective implementation of a good strategy.

Personnel and institutional conditions are essential for effective and successful diplomacy. Let's start with the former. Diplomats are the primary executors of foreign policy strategy, so the quality of diplomatic training matters greatly. Unfortunately, we face a lot of problems in this area. The trouble starts here, as to this day there is no real diplomatic training in Hungary. According to the media, diplomatic training will finally commence in the autumn of 2020 at the University of Public Service, but today we still don't know anything about its quality and impact. This is one of the serious issues of recent decades for which we've already paid a high price, and its rectification is now urgent. Prior to the change of regime, some of the diplomats were trained in an institution called GIMO in Moscow. From a professional point of view, the students received exceedingly high-quality training, but the institution was also tasked with indoctrinating the communist bloc's future diplomats because GIMO didn't only train Soviet diplomats, but those of most countries in the communist bloc. It's no coincidence that this institution was mockingly called the Janissary College. This of course doesn't mean that all students were recruited or were made firm believers in the Soviet system or the Soviet Union itself (many became disillusioned for good with the system exactly here), but the risk of this was quite high. Not surprisingly, after the change of regime demand for this training plummeted, not only in Hungary, and in most countries – often unfounded – suspicion surrounded the former students. Since 1990, therefore, GIMO hasn't been considered as a diplomatic training provider in Hungary despite the fact that it still has Hungarian students today. The problem is that its place hasn't been taken over by another form of training.

I of course know that there are quite a few international studies courses in Hungary, and some of them are of a very high standard, but this is by no means the same as diplomatic training and is at best a good foundation-level introduction to it.

Over the past almost three decades, numerous good plans and proposals have been made to start training Hungarian diplomats – I even made a proposal myself – but due to petty and narrow-minded interests, they all unfortunately ended up in the trash. Hungarian higher education is unfortunately characterised, especially in this area, by the fact that a real iron curtain separates the academic world from practice, so training provides students with only a small amount of knowledge and preparation that can be used directly in practice.

According to my proposal, diplomatic training would be a two-year postgraduate elite training course, which would essentially take place in a practice-oriented, tutoring environment and prepare its students specifically for Hungarian diplomacy. Admission would only take place after the successful completion of a multi-stage competitive examination, and students who complete the training with the best results would be guaranteed admission to the staff of the Ministry of Foreign Affairs.

There are those who are of the opinion that a country the size of Hungary doesn't really need independent diplomatic training and that we'd be better off providing state scholarships and training our diplomats in the world's recognised diplomatic training workshops. Whilst I have no objections to training abroad, it doesn't in any way substitute the need for quality domestic training. Hungarian diplomacy, also due to our geostrategic position, has very specific tasks, interests and requirements, for which only training in Hungary can really prepare. Moreover, the task of diplomatic training isn't only to reproduce professional knowledge but also to develop the ethos that is essential for the practice of this profession. For understandable reasons, international universities and institutions don't consider it their task to develop commitment and loyalty to Hungarian statehood and the Hungarian diplomatic profession. This is why I consider the creation of high-quality Hungarian diplomatic training essential. I'm cautiously optimistic about the domestic diplomatic training that is now finally starting, and which will hopefully eliminate this decade of omission.

The diplomatic service has also recently formed a privileged, segregated caste to which the rules of entry have been constantly changing but have generally been arbitrary and opaque. Counter-selection has largely prevailed, as merit and talent haven't always been rewarded during the selection process whereas nepotism and protectionism have been present – to varying degrees, but –throughout. Although an entrance exam has generally been a condition for admission, there have always been exceptions to which this didn't apply, and indeed, often the entrance exam was the exception rather than the rule and, in some cases only served to subsequently legitimise admission made on other grounds. Additionally, entrance examination requirements were often contingent and arbitrary, with subjective elements always playing an important role. Since the change of regime, all governments have been responsible, albeit to varying degrees, for ensuring that the rules of pure competition didn't apply during admission. This had the consequence that not necessarily the most talented or the most suitable were chosen to represent our country in the world. This problem was only compounded by the fact that the attractiveness of a career in diplomacy has been greatly reduced for a number of reasons. For a long time, one of the attractions of such a career was provided by financial opportunities. In contrast, today, compared to many other careers a diplomatic career isn't particularly financially attractive (this was quite different before 1990). Undoubtedly, it's also a disadvantageous profession in terms of personal relationships. According to the classical model, a diplomat's partner was a housewife, but very few today imagine their future this way. On the other hand, the profession is now completely politicised and corrupt, which also deters many.

Any system which isn't purely based on merit and performance is a corrupt system, and the less it's based on these, the more corrupt it is. I use the term corrupt in the original sense of the word; that is, I call it a tainted system. Unfortunately, diplomacy in our country suffered from this disease from the very first moment following the change of regime, and today it has become completely riddled by it.

Decisions which determine the long-term career prospects of employees, and perhaps even their fate, are made much more often in the Ministry of Foreign Affairs than in other ministries. It's by no means irrelevant who is deployed where, who gets a foreign posting (a diplomat who hasn't been in foreign service yet isn't even a real diplomat), at what rank they're deployed, as well as how, and how quickly they advance within the hierarchy. These are existential decisions which repeat themselves with great frequency. The system as a whole is determined by the criteria on which these decisions are made; solely on a professional basis, or on the basis of other criteria. Unfortunately there has always been a strong tendency in foreign affairs to favour non-professional aspects, but this has recently risen to a critical level. It appears to the outsider (but also looks the same from the inside) that the most important aspect of selection and advancement today is loyalty and connections. This unfortunately has extremely serious and negative consequences in terms of the quality and performance of diplomatic activity. This isn't just because a large number of unsuitable, unprepared people end up in the diplomatic service or important positions, which in itself is a luxury we can't afford. Perhaps even more troubling is the effect that this practice has in destroying the morale of the diplomatic service. This is because it also encourages those who are professionally suitable to set aside their professional conscience and adapt and conform to the norms (loyalty) expected by their superiors. Internal professional judgment, adjustment, and self-correction have thus been virtually eliminated and replaced by a servile mentality of blindly carrying out orders. It's like experiencing a journey into the past. The practice of the One-party-state; direct party control and loyalty to the government, has been revived. This is also faithfully expressed in the amendment to the law, which has already given civil servants official government-employee status.

Diplomats don't represent the government, though, but their country. They are of course loyal to whoever the government is at the time, but not to a particular government, and especially not to a particular party, but to their country.

Many see the presence of political appointees in the diplomatic service as constituting an element of corruption. I'm open-minded when it comes to this. There are many different practices in the world. In many countries, diplomacy is purely made up of civil servants (e.g., the British system). There are those where political appointees are rare exceptions (e.g. the Germans, the Dutch) and some where it's common practice (e.g., in the U.S.). Following the change of regime, a mixed system has become commonplace in all the countries of transition, for very understandable reasons. The new elite was suspicious of the former party-state diplomacy, considered its members unreliable, and therefore very often appointed political appointees to leadership and ambassadorial positions. After a while, several countries returned to the civil service system, whilst elsewhere there are very limited numbers of political appointees (e.g., Slovenia). Some countries have maintained a system of having more political appointees in leadership and ambassadorial positions, and there are some where they're almost exclusively political appointments (unfortunately these now include Hungary).

I'm not completely against political appointments, provided they're also based on professional considerations. In my interpretation a political appointment is acceptable or even desirable if it has a clear added value; i.e., it can be justified not only by professional arguments, but if the person appointed possesses knowledge, a system of contacts, international recognition and authority that can be put to good use for the country. Many view political appointees as incompetent dilettantes, and unfortunately many appointees have given credence to this. I of course don't support the appointment of incompetents either, but there are also plenty of good examples. In the posts of ambassador to Washington, most of the countries in transition had politically appointed ambassadors, some of whom performed outstandingly: Alexander Vondra (former Presidential Adviser and Foreign Minister) of the Czech Republic, Martin Butora (Political and Presidential Adviser) of the Slovak Republic, and Dmitry Rupel (former Foreign Minister, mayor) of Slovenia, were very well-known ambassadors to Washington, but Hungarians Géza Jeszenszky and Réka Szemerkényi also made a significant contribution to the performance of our embassy.

It's important that the number of political appointees doesn't exceed a certain – preferably not too high – proportion (in Slovenia, the law stipulates how many political appointees can be in the foreign service at one time). If there are too many, the balance may shift to the detriment of professional activity, and issues that would otherwise require professional handling will also be politicised. If many important positions are filled by political appointees, it can demotivate the staff because it sends a message that these positions are inaccessible to civil servants, and that their prospects of promotion are non-existent, or at least severely limited. One of the most important means of encouragement in diplomacy is when diplomats can see desirable career goals in front of them.

The current system is distorted and isn't sustainable from either a professional or fairness perspective. If the country is to have a competent foreign affairs leadership, which I sincerely hope will, it will most certainly remedy these problems that severely limit performance.

An appropriate institutional background is an essential condition for successful diplomacy. Here, too, there will be work aplenty for a future leadership that considers optimal operation to be important. Let's start with the ideal size. At present, Hungary has roughly a hundred and ten diplomatic missions around the world (embassies, consulate-generals, and consulates). This more or less corresponds to the number of foreign missions of similarly sized developed countries. So, this number is neither inflated nor incomprehensibly low. The great powers have global interests, and it's thus understandable that they're present everywhere or almost everywhere. This isn't justifiable in our case. It's evident that we require a presence in the major capitals, everywhere in the region, and in countries where our political and economic interests necessitate it. The truth is that the existing network could seriously do with a thorough assessment. We probably wouldn't find convincing arguments for our presence in all instances, but at the same time it might make sense to open a foreign mission in other countries or cities. Unfortunately, even in recent decades, often improvised, ill-considered decisions have been made regarding closures (e.g., Estonia) or openings, without a comprehensive impact assessment preceding the decisions. In most cases, closures were forced by financial or budget constraints, and non-professional analysis.

The Ministry of Foreign Affairs has a self-interest in continuous organisational growth, therefore there are plenty of arguments for the retention of all existing stations and for opening new ones. Yet often diplomats themselves see the impracticability of maintaining a station. In an honest conversation years ago, the Portuguese ambassador to Ljubljana told me that he'd already spent four years in Slovenia, felt great, and was happy to be there, but during those four years he failed to understand why it was worth Portugal maintaining an embassy in Ljubljana. A few years after his departure, his superiors also realised this and closed their embassy. I think in some places, we too, could do this. This is especially true for some of the stations opened in recent years.

Diplomacy is an expensive business; it costs a lot to maintain. What may seem from the outside to be flashy, an unnecessary and ostentatious waste of money, often serves an indispensable function. We'd be better served by a slightly reduced but properly equipped network than one which is swollen but treading water. Given that one of the prime tasks of diplomacy is to build the country's image and strengthen the country's prestige, this is difficult to achieve free from cost or with a small budget. This is what embassy programmes, exhibitions, conferences, and presentations serve, all of which cost money. In good instances, receptions, embassy dinners and cocktail parties aren't empty, boring, superficial social events but important venues for networking, exchanging information, and building the country's image. Underfunded embassies can't perform these tasks, so if there's a persistent lack of money for reasonably funding a larger network, it's advisable to consider operating a reduced one but with adequate funding.

One of the serious disadvantages of Hungarian diplomacy is that its institutional memory is highly incomplete and limited. This is partly related to the lack of continuity and the large-scale staff turnover, but there are also technical reasons for this. In this age of digitization the accumulated knowledge of recent decades still isn't available in digital form, and the management of existing electronically stored material isn't solved by modern search-engine software. Good old paper-based information is still one of the main knowledge bases. It's an almost insurmountable task to find out about a partner, if a Hungarian diplomat has ever met them in another country, concerning another matter, what was said then, and with whom they were in contact. If we're lucky, we know about a politician in a given country, and what our embassy reported about them, but if they were posted in another country years previously and there's a report on this, it can usually only be unearthed with great difficulty. Not to mention the elephant in the room; that is, unprocessed, encrypted telegrams. Although telegrams from recent years can now be retrieved on the basis of a few call key words, non-call content will slowly become obsolete. Information is the holy grail of effective modern diplomacy, but we unfortunately treat this treasure very carelessly. We make a great effort to obtain it, but then let it fall into obscurity.

It's a prerequisite for a well-functioning Ministry of Foreign Affairs to have a background institution for forming strategy, planning, and conducting analysis, which isn't directly part of the Ministry (i.e., not a department), has a certain degree of institutional autonomy, but is organisationally connected to the Ministry, and the information flow. It would be obvious that this role would be played by the long-standing Institute for Foreign Affairs (now known as the Institute for Foreign Affairs and Trade). Unfortunately, this institute has recently never carried out this important function, and in truth there was no need for it to do so. At the same time, this is a prime example of the intellectual paucity of Hungarian foreign policy. Additionally, at the end of 2016, the institute ceased to exist as an independent concern, and it now carries out its limited activities as a subordinate department of the Centre for Democracy Public Foundation. This decision is an excellent illustration of the current foreign affairs leadership's negligible reliance on a serious professional foundation for its decisions. At present, the formerly independent institute primarily organises events, and deals with the writing and publication of studies only loosely related to the activities of the Ministry of Foreign Affairs. It's true that important decisions aren't even made in the Ministry of Foreign Affairs, so if it were more closely linked to the ministry it wouldn't have a substantially greater role in preparing the actual decisions. This isn't even expected of it today, its task instead being to justify decisions after they've been made.

In a future healthy institutional structure, a re-established genuine Institute for Foreign Affairs must receive a key role in strategy-forming, decision-making and strategic analysis. It's important that this institute is at the same time a joint workshop for academic researchers and diplomats receptive to theoretical work, ensuring [employee] passage between the Institute and the ministry. It thus won't be merely a convalescent home for ambassadors between postings, but instead a career stepping-stone for the best-prepared diplomats.

Finally, we need to talk about the place of economic diplomacy and foreign trade in the Hungarian institutional system. In modern diplomacy – unlike in classical diplomacy –, economic diplomacy has played an important role. The primary task of diplomacy is to represent and promote the country's economic and trade policy interests. The task of diplomacy is to provide a favourable political, legal and social environment for the assertion of our foreign economic interests. Figuratively speaking, we could say that economic diplomacy opens the door to businesspeople, but its they who have to step over the threshold.

This close intertwining is also evidenced by the fact that in many countries the Ministry of Foreign Affairs has also become responsible for trade policy and investment promotion. This endeavour isn't new to us either. I, too, was involved in the struggle already in 1994 for the Ministry of Foreign Affairs to gain control over economic diplomacy. This attempt, unfortunately, wasn't successful at the time. The attempt to do so is both legitimate and right, and it's fortunate that the principle of unified foreign interest representation is no longer being questioned by anyone. After 2014, however, we went from one extreme to the other. The ministry's name already referred to this unusual shift in emphasis, it being renamed as the Ministry of Foreign Affairs and Trade by the new leaders. The Minister of Foreign Affairs and Trade, Péter Szíjjártó, has stated on countless occasions – and in this Prime Minister Viktor Orbán backed him up – that the most important, almost exclusive task of the ministry is foreign trade activity, and also announced that time was up for traditional diplomacy. The trouble with this isn't just that it has violated our traditions and the sensitivity and professional identity of diplomats, but that in this exaggerated form, it is a clearly flawed goal.

Our political and economic interests aren't always in sink. Subordinating political interests to temporary economic interests can cause very serious damage in the long run. We could cite many examples of this in recent times. The sanctions against Russia are economically harmful but violating them or just constantly calling for the lifting of the sanctions, will cause very serious damage to our reputation with our allies and to the country's predictability, which could later backfire multiple times due to other matters.

Certainly, the release of Ramil Safarov, the Azerbaijani sentenced to life imprisonment for brutally murdering one of his Armenian colleagues in Budapest with an axe, may have been driven by a narrow-minded economic calculation. It's another question that this move still hasn't paid economic dividends but has caused very serious political damage. Diplomatic relations with Armenia haven't returned to normal since then. It's no coincidence that the foreign affairs leadership at the time opposed this decision.

The great transformation of 2014 was followed by wholesale changes. Almost everywhere, "foreign trade attachés" were appointed; 128 attachés for exactly 110 stations, 50 of whom came from the outside, and the rest recruited from among former commercial and trade attachés and councillors. The responsibilities of the new foreign trade attachés were – as opposed to those of the former attachés and advisors dealing with classical trade diplomacy – extended to include not only diplomatic-, but also specifically trade related tasks too. They were thus no longer expected not only to open the door, but also to step through. Their brief covers everything that was previously the remit of businesspeople; from market research to acquiring a business and, sometimes participating in a deal. One of the problems with this is that most of them have no experience or knowledge in this field, and were thus expected to do something which, despite their best intentions, lay beyond their abilities. The other problem is that in the meantime, they were members of a bureaucratic organisation, had many bureaucratic obligations, and their rewards and career advancements weren't decided by the clients but by people who made decisions based on reports and compliance with protocol obligations rather than actual effectiveness. It's always problematic if a service provider isn't fundamentally dependent on the people whose benefit it provides the service for, because then it optimises performance not according to the customer, but according to management expectations. In any case, it's unfortunate and, not permissible under international law to confuse diplomatic and direct commercial activities.

This problem could have been solved through chambers of commerce. This can't be considered a success story either, it being no surprise that the 14 chambers of commerce launched amidst high hopes for the Southern Opening were already closed by 2017, but this was only a precursor to the announced closure, in summer 2018, of the national trading network covering 41 countries. Magyar Nemzeti Kereskedőház Zrt. was wound up at the same time and merged into the Hungarian Export Promotion Agency (HEPA), which established seven regional centres, and operates more purposefully than before.

These measures also constitute an acknowledgement of the complete failure of the original concept, although there's no doubt that the basic idea is correct. It's necessary to support the foreign business activities of Hungarian-owned small and medium-sized enterprises, because they aren't, or only to a very limited extent, capable of doing so on their own. Large Hungarian companies and regional champions (MOL, OTP, Richter, etc.) don't need this, given that they have their own foreign representatives and partner agencies, and this is even more true for multinational corporate giants which are also present in Hungary.

Nor can it be disputed that this area is eligible for state aid and, if the chambers of commerce had done their job well, it would have paid off in the long run not only for the companies concerned, but also for taxpayers. The activities of chambers of commerce can be really effective if they operate entirely on a market-oriented basis. That is, if they aren't managed by a state-owned company under ministerial supervision, but by the stakeholders' representative body representing their own interests, or by bodies representing various different interests. This could be a chamber based on the Austrian model, but other business interest groups could also be involved in the maintenance and management. The activity can of course also be supported from taxpayers' money, albeit alongside a significant contribution from those concerned as well as from the direct beneficiaries.

Services provided free of charge, even psychotherapy, aren't not worth much. Neither the recipient nor the provider attaches much value to them. Additionally, if the beneficiary doesn't pay anything for the service, they can't really count on the quality

175

of service they receive. Here, in addition to sticking to the objective and activities, a fundamental change of approach, and institutional reform, are required in order for Hungarian small and medium-sized enterprises to receive effective business and market support. It's important to clearly separate the activities of the chambers of commerce and the trade attachés. Duplication is harmful, costs twice as much, and ends up causing only confusion, leading to the pinning of responsibility on others, as well as a blame game.

In conclusion, a process has started in this area which can be later relied upon but, in its present form, a costly, inefficient, confusing institutional solution has emerged. A clear situation must be created were everyone knows their task. Diplomats should deal with trade diplomacy, trade policy, and investment promotion, whilst the Hungarian Export Promotion Agency, replacing the chambers of commerce, should provide specific partner search, market research, business and legal advice, further training, and so forth, for Hungarian small and medium-sized enterprises.

In place of a conclusion

The writing of this book was preceded by a long gap. I'd been toying with the idea for years, but had a hard time devoting myself to it. Will there be a market for my book, will it have an audience, or will it disappear without trace in the sea of unnecessarily written books? Many people encouraged and emboldened me to do so, but is that enough to make the book worth writing and publishing? To this day I don't know the reassuring answer to these doubts.

Over time, the feeling that I had no right to keep to myself that which I have presented in this book, grew stronger and eventually overwhelmed me. Readers will decide for themselves if they have a need for it; I can't make that decision for them. I owe this book to my career, my contemporaries, my mentors, and my compatriots who hold an interest in matters of public life, who are interested in our country's foreign policy, its renewal, and a possible strategic vision.

I've been working professionally in foreign affairs for three decades now. This used to be called a lifetime. From among those intellectuals who were also interested in foreign policy, I held only a moderate enthusiasm; it rather being circumstances that dictated I carve out a career in foreign affairs. In the autumn of 1988, members of the newly formed SZDSZ (Alliance of Free Democrats) allocated themselves roles in the various competencies. The greatest scramble was, understandably, for those covering domestic political issues, and the foreign affairs post remained unfilled. At the strong encouragement of Bálint Magyar I took on the role of being the party's person responsible for foreign affairs. I can't deny that I was a little reluctant at first, given that at the time of the regime change, all the other tasks appeared more exciting and important than foreign policy. Today, I'm grateful for the choice that has defined the subsequent three decades of my life up until now. It led directly to me becoming First Secretary, and then Vice-Chairman of the Foreign affairs Committee of the first freely elected parliament. In the second parliamentary cycle I was Political Secretary of State in the Ministry for Foreign Affairs, then Chairman of the parliament's Foreign Affairs Committee and, a term later, of the Committee on European Integration. In these roles I was able to take an active part in the development and implementation of the 'good neighbours' policy, I participated in the NATO accession process, I played an active role in the preparation for accession to the EU, and in the early days of Hungary being a member state. I participated in the process of drafting the European Constitution as a supplementary member of the European Convention, where I also worked primarily in the working party on Foreign Affairs and Defence. I had the honour of being one of the first Hungarian members of the European Parliament, where I dealt primarily with foreign policy, human rights and minority protection issues. After the end of my term of office, I served as Ambassador to neighbouring Slovenia for five years, and then as a foreign policy analyst and consultant, I remained in close contact with the field of foreign affairs.

I don't write all this in order to boast, merely as a testimony that I've spent three decades visiting almost all the important corridors of power (the Hungarian Parliament, government, European Parliament, diplomacy) when holding positions of responsibility, during which I've come across all sorts of situations and been enriched by many different experiences. Do I have the right to keep all this to myself and not give back, at least in part, to those whose trust and support I have trodden this walk of life with?

The long and short of it is that I wrote this book. I chose not to write a memoir, and there are two reasons for this. On the one hand, I don't feel that I've reached the end of my career (when I'll be reliving my memories), and on the other hand, I'm also averse to the genre because it often tempts you to start building a monument to yourself, and didn't at all want that. Neither did I wish to write a monograph, or an academic study – namely because I want to address a much wider audience than the narrow readership of chunky academic dissertations. What I wanted to say in this book, is for everyone who's interested in Hungary's room for manoeuvre in foreign policy, its most pressing foreign policy dilemmas, its recent history, and the strategic vision of an alternative foreign policy that I consider desirable.

The genre I chose is practically unknown in Hungarian language publications, and I'd be happy if this book also contributes to its introduction in Hungary. I undertook to formulate my statements in the style of the geopolitical rapid analyses of the Anglo-Saxon world, and of think-tank policy papers. In my experience, this genre is the best fit for talking concisely, succinctly, and intelligibly about even highly complex and complicated issues. I leave it to the reader to judge how successful I've been in this endeavour.

"Books have their own destinies" so goes the Latin saying. The author has little influence on this. Every book has as many possible judgements as there are readers (let's discount those who judge a book without having read it, even though they aren't in short supply). I confidently pass this book on to my prospective readership.

I have now reached the end of my book, and in doing so I believe I've at least partially repaid the debt that let me to write it. From here on in I entrust its fate to the reader. I do hope that

I've been able to contribute to arousing interest in foreign policy and to a renewal in foreign policy thinking, even if only to a small extent.

The book's title, *Quo vadis, Hungary?* formulates a question. Where is Hungary heading? This is a reference to the *Apocryphal Acts of [Saint]Peter,* when Peter, forced to flee Rome, meets the risen Christ on the way and asks him, "Where are you going, Lord?" (Quō vādis, Domine?). Christ replies to him, "I'm going to Rome to be crucified again." (Rōmam eō iterum crucifigī). Drawing strength from this answer, Peter continues his ministry.

Peter the Apostle's question is also relevant for Hungary. For the Hungary which has today lost its compass and has taken the wrong path, just like our great national poet, Endre Ady's mythical Lost Rider. This book is a modest suggestion as to direction Hungary should go in, extracting itself from, as Ady puts it:

> Only bloodshed and mystery,
> Footprints ancestral in ancient ways,
> Only the forest, only the reeds,
> Only the madmen of vanished days.
> Lost and ancient the traveller rides,
> Through new grown brushwood upon his way,

(Translation by J.C.W. Horne)

I hope that the Lost Rider, that metaphor of old Hungary, at long last gets out of the thick bush and old reeds and finds his way. If I've succeeded in helping a little in this endeavour, then it made sense to write this book.

Printing House:
Pannónia Nyomda Kft.
1139 Budapest, Frangepán u. 16.

Printed in Great Britain
by Amazon

57451327R00108